MW00792017

Taking Men Alive

Studies in the Principles and Practise of Individual Soul-Winning

BY

CHARLES GALLAUDET TRUMBULL

"From henceforth thou shalt take men alive"
—LUKE 5:10

Wipf & Stock
PUBLISHERS
Eugene, Oregon

Wipf and Stock Publishers
199 West 8th Avenue, Suite 3
Eugene, Oregon 97401

Taking Men Alive
By Trumbell, Charles G
Copyright©1907, 1938 by Trumbell, Charles Gallaudet
ISBN: 1-57910-425-8
Publication date 12/14/1999
Previously published by Intl. Comm. of Young Men's Christian Assoc. /Fleming
Revell, 1907, 1938

FOREWORD TO NEW EDITION

MEN still need to be won to Christ. "Taking men alive" for Christ is still the chief responsibility and privilege of Christians. For if men are not "taken alive" for Christ, they will be "taken alive" for Satan; as the first chapter of this study of personal work shows, the Greek verb meaning "to take alive" occurs only twice in the New Testament, in one case meaning capturing men unto eternal life, in the other, Satan's capture of men unto eternal death.

And the best way of winning men to Christ is to lead them to him one by one. It was our Lord's own method; it was the method of his apostles; and it has been the method of the greatest soul-winners from his day until now. The beauty of this form of evangelism is that everyone can do it. Few can be great preachers, few are gifted Bible teachers; all can be, and should be, witnesses to the One who has brought them out of death into life.

It was undoubtedly the usual practice among the early Christians to tell others with whom they had daily contact in the pagan or heathen world around them, of the death and resurrection of Jesus Christ, the Son of God and Saviour of sinners, and to tell what he had done for them and what he meant to them in their personal life and experience. There is as great need of this today as in the first century—even greater. May we not make application of a part of the first verse of

Hebrews 12 and say, "Wherefore seeing we also are compassed about with so great a cloud of witnesses, let us" become witnesses ourselves to the same God and Saviour to whom they were true, and to whom we have been led because of their faithful witnessing?

It is better to tell others about Christ in a faltering or even mistaken way than not to tell them at all. Dr. Ernest M. Wadsworth, Director of The Great Commission Prayer League of Chicago, has called attention to a mistake that was made by an earnest soul-winner, long ago, named Philip. The record is in the first chapter of John's Gospel. Philip had been won to Christ by the personal work of the Lord himself. Then we read: "Philip findeth Nathanael, and saith unto him, We have found him, of whom Moses in the law, and the prophets, did write, Jesus of Nazareth, the son of Joseph." And Philip made a very serious mistake in what he said about Jesus of Nazareth. He called him "the son of Joseph," which he certainly was not. But Philip's mistake was made in good faith, unintentionally, and in an ignorance for which doubtless he was not at all to blame. Did the Lord rebuke or condemn Philip for this denial of His virgin birth? He spoke not a word of reproof, but welcomed the man Philip led to him, and doubtless welcomed Philip's devoted and earnest testimony.

One of the officials of one of our large Eastern railroads, himself a soul-winning Christian, was walking along a Philadelphia street recently when he saw an old colored man standing by the curb, offering a street vendor's wares for sale. The railroad man stepped up to him as he noticed, from something the old man was saying, that he evidently was a Christian. "I see you are in the pilgrim way," said the railroad man.

"Yes, sir," was the respectful reply.

"Would you mind telling me how you came into the pilgrim way?" asked the railroad man.

The old man set his tray down, took some worn papers from an inside coat pocket, and fumbled among them until he found what he was after, then handed it to his new friend. "This was what led me there," he said. It was a small Gospel of John. The other man opened it and looked with interest through its pages, and he saw on a flyleaf the words: "Presented to ——————— (filled in with the colored man's name) by J. Harvey Borton." The railroad man's heart leaped within him, for he knew Mr. Borton intimately as one of the leading business men of Philadelphia who, only a few months before, had been taken Home to be with the Lord. Mr. Borton is known to a host of business leaders as well as earnest Christian people throughout America, having been one of the leading Christian laymen of this country. But he thought it worth while, in his busy life of large responsibilities, to lead an old colored man and street vendor to Christ. We can all do this work if we will.

C. G. T.

November, 1938.

INTRODUCTION

O N the eighth of December, 1903, a great printing
machine was awaiting a message in type that
should carry, to the hundred thousand readers of the
paper which it was to print, the news of the death of
its editor. The one who, in that moment of grief
and uncertainty, must write the message, tried to view
the seventy-three years of life that had just closed, the
half-century of manhood that had ministered unceas-
ingly. The life was rich in varied and extended forms
of service: as home missionary in Sunday-school work,
as army chaplain, as interpreter of the Bible, as
traveler and explorer, as preacher and speaker and
editor, and as writer of more than thirty volumes in
the field of character-building and spiritual truth.

Yet in that hour when death seems to reveal the
real man and his central power and purpose, the one
form of ministry that stood out in clearest, whitest
light to those who knew this man best was the ministry of which the world at large, though it knew him
well, knew least. It was his self-sacrificing service for
the individual: his instant and invariable putting of
the claims of one above the claims of many: his sinking and spending all that he had and all that he was
in order to serve the one-at-a-time for whom he lived.

And so the message that told of the earthly ending
of his life was the message that the whole life had
spoken; and the summons was sounded, to all who

loved him, to "make his past a success" by carrying on his greatest work, the winning of individuals to Christ. And it is significant that one of the least pretentious of the thirty volumes that Henry Clay Trumbull wrote is proving to be the most influential of them all in far-reaching blessing,—the little book that tells the simple narrative of his "Individual Work for Individuals."

      *   *   *

A few months after the death of Dr. Trumbull, the writer was asked to conduct a class at the annual con-vention of the Brotherhood of Andrew and Philip, in the study of "Individual Work for Individuals," on the basis of the experiences set down by his father in the volume on that subject.

The idea of using that book as a text-book for class study was a new one, for it had not been written with just that end in view. But the wealth of material for study that it contained was unquestionable. So the experiment was tried; and every one who had a part in it was, apparently, surprised not only at the adaptability of the material to a classification by principles, but also at the definiteness and simplicity of the several principles which were clearly seen to be at the foundation of the success of the work that Dr. Trumbull did. Laymen and ministers in that summer study-class who had already been familiar with the contents of the little volume, and yet who had never sought to ascertain the principles of work which it does not specifically mention, but which it abundantly reveals, expressed themselves as impressed with the importance and the gain of this new view of the work.

In the three years that have passed since then, the writer has been privileged to test the studies of that summer, on more than a score of occasions, with both large and small audiences, in ten different states and provinces of North America. Sometimes but a single session has been devoted to the subject; again, a small group of students has met for three or four consecutive class sessions, ready for thorough-going investigation. In Brotherhood, Sunday-school, and Christian Endeavor conventions, church prayer-meetings, a men's guild, a university students' Christian association, church congregations, and theological seminaries in Pennsylvania, New Jersey, Kentucky, and Tennessee, the principles have been presented, worked out, challenged, discussed, and often unexpectedly illuminated by those who have brought their own fruitful experiences to bear. The material that has gone into the following pages is the result of these three years of study and conference.

H. Clay Trumbull's "Individual Work for Individuals" is chiefly a record of actual experiences, grouped by chronological periods in the life of its writer, and intended primarily to show what God is willing to do for one who seeks to improve daily opportunities of extending His invitation. The details of the way in which the work was done are given in that book in great fulness, but it was not the purpose of the book to make a special study or presentation of the method back of the work,—in other words, to make a specific statement of the principles underlying the art. It is easy to miss those principles unless one specifically looks for them, and, missing them, to fail in the effectiveness that one might have and ought to have. The ascertaining, formulating, and illustrating of such principles is the distinctive purpose of the present studies.

While this study of the art of " Taking Men Alive " is based upon the experiences narrated in Dr. Trumbull's volume, and quotes copiously from that work in illustration of the various principles here set forth, yet the material of that volume is by no means all given here, and those who would realize the richness of God's blessing upon consistent efforts to do this work will miss much if they fail to study the other book also. Still another work linked closely with these two in its study of methods of leading men into spiritual light is Dr. Trumbull's "How to Deal with Doubts and Doubters." It furnishes admirable supplementary work for a class that has completed the present studies.

       *   *   *

In that classic little story entitled " Fishin' Jimmy," by a sister of Dr. Trumbull's, Mrs. Annie Trumbull Slosson, the quaint old New England character whose life is Mrs. Slosson's theme has convictions on the subject of his occupation. " To his simple intellect," writes the author, "the fisherman's art was a whole system of morality, a guide for everyday life, an education, a gospel. It was all any mortal man, woman, or child, needed in this world to make him or her happy, useful, good....And he always spoke of his pursuit as one speaks of something very dear, very sacred." His first real interest in Christ was when he learned that here was " Some One that was dreffle fond o' fishin' an' fishermen, Some One that sot everythin' by the water, an' useter go along by the lakes an' ponds, an' sail on 'em, an' talk with the men that was fishin'. An' how the fishermen all liked him, 'nd asked his 'dvice, an' done jest 's he telled 'em about the likeliest places to fish; an' how they allers ketched more for mindin' him....An' so fust thing I knowed I says to myself, 'That's the kind o' teacher I want. If I could come acrost a man like that, I'd jest foller him, too, through thick an' thin....I tell ye, his r'liging's a fishin' r'liging all through.' "

Fishin' Jimmy seemed to have the idea for which the Master Fisherman stood, and the phrase, "the art of taking men alive," may suggest both the method and the purpose of the Great Commission. The successful fisherman embodies the very characteristics which it is a duty for every soul-winner to have,— and that ought to mean every follower of Christ. Patience, knowledge of the interests of his fish, knowledge of the bait that will attract fish, faith in things unseen, skill, delicacy of touch, refusal to be discouraged, unlimited perseverance, conviction that he has not yet exhausted the possibilities of his art,—all these and more make the true fisherman. And it is important to note that not a single one of these essentials is beyond the power of any one to attain. If one is not a "born" fisherman, he can learn how; and he ought. Christ's demands are always reasonable. He never enjoins the impossible without making it possible.

Fishin' Jimmy's "wonder was never-ending that, in the scheme of evangelizing the world, more use was not made of the ' fishin' side ' of the story. 'Haint they ever tried it on them poor heathen?' he would ask earnestly....' I should think 'twould 'a' ben the fust thing they'd done. *Fishin' fust, an' r'liging's sure to foller.'* "

CONTENTS

The footnotes throughout the book, except when otherwise indicated, refer to pages in H. Clay Trumbull's "Individual Work for Individuals." They are given simply for the convenience of readers who may wish to locate the original passages.

Bible passages are usually quoted from the American Standard Revision.

I. THE WORK WE ARE FACING

II. THE WORKER AND HIS EQUIPMENT

Contents

HINTS TO CLASS LEADERS

WHILE the plan of this book is such that it may easily be used for reading without special study, or again for home study by an individual alone, it is the hope of its publishers and author that it will find its widest usefulness in class use, as a text-book for small or large groups of persons, in the local church and young people's society, in summer schools and assemblies, in Young Men's Christian Associations, in student conferences and college association work, and in the theological seminaries. No individual study of this theme can hope to compare in richness of result with the study that one does in a group of interested workers and thinkers, whose experiences and opinions, brought out in free, informal conference, are sure to stimulate all to fuller understanding, keener enthusiasm, and deeper conviction.

The class group need not necessarily be large. Do not defer the formation of a class because there are "not enough." Do not be discouraged if only a few, because of rain or some other such factor, attend a meeting which promised to be larger. The rain-tested few are worth more than the fair-weather many. It was a favorite belief—half-joking, half-serious—of H. Clay Trumbull's, that in any public meeting there is just about so much good to go around, therefore the fewer there are present, the more each one is likely to get. A group of two or three earnest souls may

gain more from their study than a class of twenty
or thirty less genuinely interested students. The small
group always has certain advantages over the large,
in its informality and unity of spirit, the opportunity
of each member to take greater part in the sessions,
and the opportunity which the leader has of coming
close to each member. Yet if a considerable number
is available for a class, that fact is to be welcomed,
and a leader who is determined to be really a leader,
not a lecturer or preacher or other monopolist of the
time and subject, can see to it that the large number
does not prevent free expression by members of the
class.

Getting the Students to Work

The wise and skilful leader will invariably do less
talking than his class does. He will resolutely make
every session a *conference,*—a time when the class
members and the leader confer freely with each other
over the problems and truths, the principles and the
methods, that are before them for that day. An en-
thusiastic leader may *tell* a class a great deal of interesting information, but if he does not get it back
again from them, by the giving out of questions and
opinions and experiences on their part, he will have
taught them little or nothing.

For thorough work, every member of the class
will have his or her own copy of this text-book, and
a note-book. The questions and suggestions that
appear at the beginning and the end of every chapter
furnish material which the leader can readily use,
if he so desires. For example, while every member
of the class should, for the best results, study the

"Preparatory Thoughts and Questions" that introduce each chapter (being careful to do so *before* reading a word of the chapter), the leader may profitably
assign certain of these preparatory questions, in advance, to different members, they to report upon them
in class at the beginning of the session in which that
chapter is to be studied.

Thus, at the close of the session during which
Chapter I has been studied, the leader may assign
respectively to different students certain of the questions that introduce Chapter II, asking them to study
and write out their answers at home before reading
Chapter II, and bring those answers into class with
them at the next session. Of course, the reading of a
chapter may materially modify or entirely reverse one's
preconceived opinions on a given point, but that fact
will only make this part of the home study, and of
the class session, the more interesting.

Again, two members might be assigned the same
preparatory question to report upon, so that the class
may compare the results. Or in some instances the
leader might ask the entire class to report on the same
question or questions, thus insuring an interesting and
profitable variety of views for consideration.

The great thing is to get the student to *do his own
thinking*. That is the purpose of those preparatory
questions, and it should be the ever-present purpose
of the true leader. It can be accomplished in number-
less ways, some of which each leader will work out
for himself. But unless it is accomplished, the results of any study of this subject will fall far short
of what they might be.

If each member has his own book, all will read

and study at home, in preparation for a lesson, such chapter or chapters as the leader may assign for the coming session of the class. The questions and topics at the end of each chapter will suggest to the leader how to test his class's knowledge of the contents of that chapter.

Urge the students to answer the questions at the end of the chapters, whether at home or in class, largely in their own words rather than in the words of the book, seeking to catch the ideas and principles presented in the book so fully that they can express them readily in their own language. Then they will have made them their own.

It will be noted that certain of the questions or topics at the ends of chapters are not strictly confined to the contents of that chapter, but call for original work, and thus furnish additional material for assigning in advance for the students' home work, when that is desired.

Actual Soul-Winning Between Sessions

The class that is content to let its study of this theme be purely theoretical might better not study at all. Every class should be a training school for service, and every student should be hard at work in that service between sessions. The most profitable feature of class work ought to be the study, by the class, of those actual experiences in individual soul-winning which members are having between sessions, and which they report in full to the class. Let the circumstances of such cases be carefully described, with the results so far as seen, and let the class discuss the special difficulties that characterize them, the problems involved, and the methods that have been or ought to be used in dealing with them. The class session will thus have a laboratory or clinical nature the value of which cannot be overestimated. A season of prayer for those yet unreached with whom present members have worked, and for a blessing upon the study looking toward the greater efficiency of the workers in this greatest work that Christ entrusts to men, will deepen and heighten the value of every moment of such study.

The note-books should be used freely, in class and out, by both leader and students. Questions and points that occur to one in home-study should be jotted down, for class discussion; so with problems and difficulties met with in one's personal experiences.

Conducting a Session

The method of conducting a session will, of course, be determined by every leader for himself. It is desirable, however, that each session should include the following features:

Reports by students on work assigned in advance.

A review of the principle or principles studied at the preceding session.

The statement of the principle or principles under study that day.

The illustration of such principle or principles, both out of the text-book and from the students' or others' actual experiences.

At the close of every session, as throughout, there will be free discussion and ample opportunity for the expression of honest differences of opinion.

If, for any reason it does not seem advisable to assign work to individual students in advance, the leader, instead, may devote a few minutes at the close of each session to an open discussion of the preparatory questions that introduce the chapter which is to be studied at the following session. This will stimulate interest in the coming lesson, and has the advantage of calling out the uninfluenced thoughts of the class on the principles that are to be studied later.

Encourage the members of the class to ask questions freely, to tell of their own experiences and difficulties, their problems and their victories in this work. Let it be understood not only that they need not hesitate to interrupt the leader when he is talking, but that there is no such thing as an "interruption" in that class: that every such interruption is a contribution to the very end for which the class exists.

Encouraging Original Work

Original work by the members of the class is to be encouraged at every opportunity. Suggest their discovering other principles of successful soul-winning, in addition to those given in this book, by their own independent study of these or other experiences. The author will appreciate it if both leaders and members of classes will have in mind his request as given on page 191. Particularly should original study be done in connection with Chapter IX, "How Our Lord Worked." That chapter is not intended to be at all exhaustive. It only suggests how readily these principles of soul-winning may be tested by our Lord's work and teachings. There is a wealth of opportunity to discover unworked material in this same line in the Gospels, which any class or student that is in earnest can well take advantage of.

How Many Sessions ?

The number of sessions that a class devotes to the study of this volume need not necessarily be the number of chapters in the book, ten, though that offers a course of reasonable length. Some chapters are much shorter than others,—such as Chapters III, VI, and X,—and might be combined with other chapters in single lessons by those who desire to shorten the time of the course. If a class wished to cover the ground in as few as four lessons, for example, the following combinations of chapters would be advisable:

Lesson I.—Chapters I, II, III.

Lesson II.—Chapters IV, V, VI.

Lesson III.—Chapters VII, VIII.

Lesson IV.—Chapters IX, X.

A course of six lessons would consist of the following groups: I; II, III; IV, V; VI, VII; VIII; IX, X.

But for a class that is willing to devote ample time to these studies, a session of a full hour can profitably be given to each of the chapters (with the possible exception of III, which is vital but not time-consuming, and which could be joined with II), provided the general plan of preparation and the conduct of the session already outlined be carried out.

Making It Personal

It is often an impressive and memorable object-lesson, when conducting any public meeting or class on this subject, to ask those to rise who were won by a sermon or a general appeal to take the final step in open confession of Christ as Saviour; then to ask those to rise who were led to that step by the face-to-face, individual word of some individual.[1]   This is likely, in any small group or large audience of Christian people, to demonstrate convincingly the place of individual soul-winning as the great factor in the extension of the Kingdom on earth.

[1] See pages 41-42 of this volume.

THE WORK WE ARE FACING

(For study before reading this chapter)

1. What is individual soul-winning? Formulate your own careful definition.
2. For whom is it a duty? Why?
3. From your own observation, what percentage of church members should you say engage in it?
4. As between minister and layman, who has the better opportunity to carry on this work?
5. Is the greatest proficiency in the work acquired, or a gift?
6. What form of Christian service would you consider greater than this?
7. To what facts and factors do you attribute the peculiar effectiveness of individual work?

1

THE WORK WE ARE FACING

IF Jesus of Nazareth had not been a Master Fisherman, the work of extending his Kingdom among men would have ended with his death. If we do not learn and practise his art of fishing, or "taking men alive," we shall be failures in the chief work of his Kingdom on earth.

And the fishing unto eternal life must be done individually. Let us therefore consider at the outset these three truths:

The work of individual soul-winning is the greatest work that God permits men to do.

It was Christ's own preferred method of work, as it is his preferred method for us to-day. For it is always the most effective way of working.

It is the hardest work in the world to do, and it always will be the hardest.

If we are not prepared to accept these statements as true, we shall have opportunity to investigate and test them as we go on with our studies. But, let us remember, every man in the world is going to be " taken alive "—by some one. The Greek *zogreo,* meaning " to take alive," occurs only twice in the entire New Testament: in Luke 5: 10, and 2 Timothy 2: 26. In the one case Jesus promises to enable his

disciple to take men alive for the Kingdom. In the
other case, Paul speaks of those who have been taken
alive by the Devil. It is the same word in both cases,
but with what a different outcome! By one or the
other fisher of men every soul will eventually be taken,
—taken alive unto death, or taken alive unto eternal
life.

The basis of these studies will be the record of the
experiences that one man had during fifty years of
work as an individual soul-winner.[1] He seemed to
have peculiar power and to be blessed with exceptional
success in the work. Why was this? What was the
secret of his power? Was it a gift that can be possessed only by a few? Or did he work in accordance
with well-defined and plainly-recognizable principles,
which any one may apply who is willing to pay the
price in study and practise, and the application of
which is as sure to bring results as the application of
the principles of any other art? These are questions
which it is the purpose of these studies to answer.

For one thing, let us note that this man was a layman throughout his life, and therefore that he had no
professional equipment such as the ordinary Christian
worker lacks. He had the degree of D.D., to be sure,
but that was purely honorary. He never was inside a
theological seminary in his life, except as a visitor.
He never even went to college. He had a rudimentary
school education, and not much of that after fourteen
years of age. He was put hard at work in the school

[1] "Individual Work for Individuals: a Record of Personal Expe
riences and Convictions." By H. Clay Trumbull. (New York: The
International Committee of Young Men's Christian Associations.)
The footnotes given hereafter refer to pages in that book, except when
they refer to other sources as indicated, or to other parts of the present volume.

of life early,—and that school is open to us all. He worked always and only as a man among men, never from any vantage point of professional or pulpit position. Even when performing the duties of an ordained army chaplain, he worked as a layman rather than as a chaplain:

> The Christian work that told [in the army] was not that of address to a collection of persons, but the man-to-man appeal of the chaplain to the single officer or soldier, when no one else was within sight or hearing. And this advantage was not because the chaplain was a chaplain, and therefore he had to work in a peculiar way, but it was because the chaplain was a man and his charge was made up of individual men, and his best way to deal with his men was the best way to deal with all men.[1]

But he had a secret of success. He learned, amid the hard knocks of political and business life, and later as a Sunday-school missionary and an army chaplain, that men are to be won in any field, whether that of merchandise, life-insurance, or soul-salvation, only in accordance with certain definite principles of man-winning. He *had* to learn what those principles were, or fail throughout. And he applied them to this chief business of life, as well as to its side-issues.

Individual Work the Greatest Work

That individual soul-winning is the greatest work that God calls men to do is simply part of the paradox-principle that runs through the entire Bible. A paradox is a seeming contradiction. We begin to meet it as soon as we begin to study the Bible. For there is a paradox at the very heart of things. The Way of

[1] Pages 28-29.

Life is the great paradox of the universe. Here it is:
*Whosoever would save his life shall lose it; but who-
soever shall lose his life for my sake, the same shall
save it.*[1] The Man who was to win the world must
do so by being rejected of the world. He who saves
from death by conquering death does so by himself
yielding to death. *He that is least among you all, the
same is great.*[2] It is the sacrifice of the greater for
the lesser, the worthy for the unworthy, the strong for
the weak; not the loveless theory of the survival of
the fittest, but instead the sacrifice of the fittest that
the feeblest may survive. So it goes. The place of the
paradox, or the seeming inversion of the natural order,
is so firmly rooted in all our Christian life and studies
that it needs no argument or proof.

That one is more than many is simply in line with
this eternal principle. You cannot reach a thousand
unless you can reach one. The greatest preaching in
the world is the preaching to an individual. The world
is never going to be brought to Christ wholesale, but
one by one. Men are not born collectively; they do not
die collectively; they do not accept or reject Christ
collectively.

But it is not yet recognized as generally as it should
be that the leading of a single soul to Christ is rarely
accomplished by a general or a pulpit appeal.

It is not enough for us to cry out a message to those
who may hear, or who may not; to those who may understand it, or who may not. We have a hearer to win as
well as a hearer to proclaim to. As Dr. Duryea forcibly put
it, "The sick soul needs not a lecture on medicine, but a prescription." Has not the ordinary method of the physician

[1] Luke 9: 24.   [2] Luke 9: 48.

of souls been that of a lecturer rather than of a prescriber? Is this the proper, or the sensible way? This volume advocates the methods of wise personal prescription for the sick soul.[1]

General preaching has its place; but it is a preliminary only in this work; the harvest must be hand-picked.

A stationary fog-horn has its value on a reef, or a rocky shore, as a warning to those who approach the point of danger. We must not say that this mode of sounding an alarm has no value, but we cannot suppose that a fog-horn, however clear its sound or well worked its mechanism, can fill the place of a coast guard of trained life-savers, who are on the watch to put out with their well-manned life-boat to save endangered single souls.[2]

The strongest preachers are unhesitating in their conviction as to the primary importance of individual work.

As a rule, the intensity of the appeal is in inverse proportion to the area covered; in other words, the greater your audience, the smaller the probability of your appeal coming home to a single heart. I once heard Henry Ward Beecher say, " The longer I live, the more confidence I have in those sermons preached where one man is the minister and one man is the congregation; where there's no question as to who is meant when the preacher says, ' Thou art the man.'" Years after this, I heard the Rev. Dr. Nevius speak similarly as to the missionary field in China. He said he wanted no great preachers in his field. That was not the sort of missionaries who were needed in China. If he could find a man who could talk familiarly, face to face, with another man, wherever he met him, he had missionary work for that kind of man in China. This is the way to do Christian work in China, or in America.[3]

Such a man as Mr. Moody, who thought more of how many individual souls he could reach than of his preaching before any audience, however large, was always desirous of getting through with his preparatory pulpit appeal and of getting at his more important work of pleading with individual souls in the inquiry meeting. And that is the feeling of every earnest evangelist who thinks more of the work of reaping and harvesting than of the work of incessantly sowing broadcast seed that may, or that may not, have final fruitage.[1]

It is not merely that individual work is a helpful addition to other work of the minister, but that it is the chief work, and that from it come strength and power for other work. Such a minister as Dr. Maltbie D. Babcock was a memorable witness to this truth. A college student wrote of him:

Outside of our circle, little has been known of Dr. Babcock's wonderful influence upon the lives of American students. Among us his work was a quiet one. Our fears, our hopes, our ambitions, were told him, and we were comforted, advised, enthused, by him; but his lips were safe keepers, and our struggles were known only to him. Especially to the students of the [John] Hopkins University, of the Woman's College, and of the other educational institutions of Baltimore, Dr. Babcock was a friend and adviser. To many, in fact, to most people, we were known as a *body*, as students of this or that institution,—to Dr. Babcock we were known as *individuals*. He knew our faces, our names, our peculiar experiences, and from him we each received personal attention.[2]

The absolute unselfishness of the man was an ever-new lesson, even to those who knew him best. One morning one of his congregation called, about nine o'clock, to see him. Finding him just finishing breakfast, he twitted him on being a late riser.

"Come, now," said Dr. Babcock, "I believe I was up earlier than you this morning."

[1] Pages 8-9.
[2] From The Sunday School Times of January 4, 1903.

"Well, what time was it?"

"Four o'clock," was the reply.

"What do you mean?" asked the astonished visitor.

"Oh, well! I had to run out to see a sick girl who lived some distance off; they sent for me," Dr. Babcock explained.

"Do you mean you got up at four o'clock in the morning to visit a sick girl who wanted to see you? Why, that's as bad as being a physician!"

"Nonsense," said the pastor; "I've gotten up many a time earlier than that to go fishing, and been proud of it. Can't I do as much for a sick girl?"

And that put an end to the matter.[1]

One afternoon he found himself in the neighborhood of a very large hardware store, and, remembering a number of articles of which he had need, entered. The clerks were probably busy, and doubtless inattentive. He waited a few minutes, and no one took notice of him. Instead of going out in vexation, or rebuking them, he stepped to a shifting-ladder on one side, and, mounting it, took from a box several articles he desired, and placed them on the counter; then rolling the ladder along a little, he ascended again and got other articles, depositing them as before. This he repeated. When getting them together, he sought, and at length secured, the attention of one of the clerks, who came forward, no doubt a little ashamed of the treatment the stranger had received, and evidently in no very agreeable mood.

"I want these articles. How much will they be?"

"Two dollars and a half" (very groutily).

"Well, you may send them to the Rev. M. D. Babcock, 14 East Thirty-seventh Street. And, now, what is your name?"

(Clerk, sulky and apprehensive) "Bradley."

"And what is your first name?"

(Unwillingly, slowly) "Charles."

"May I ask you one other question,—do you go to church?"

"No, I'm no church-goer."

(Dr. Babcock, putting his hand pleasantly on the clerk's

[1] From The Sunday School Times of May 25, 1901.

shoulder, and with enthusiasm) " Now, Charlie, I want you to
come down to my church, Fifth Avenue and Thirty-seventh
Street, next Sunday. I shall preach, and I shall be real glad
to see you. I shall have an eye out for you."

The next Sunday " Charlie " came with one or two of
his friends, and the Sunday after that every clerk in the
establishment came, and continued to come from that time.

But for the " love " which " is not easily provoked," and
which " seeketh not her own," such a result could not have
been possible.

" How can the church reach the masses?" Does not such
a life as Maltbie Babcock's give the best answer?[1]

And which would any sensible pastor and preacher
choose for his own church if it were merely a matter
of choice; to have great revival meetings, or to have
every church member actively and persistently engaged in individual soul-winning seven days in the
week all the year round? The second would insure the
first; but the first, unfortunately, occurs without being
followed by the second.

Individual Work Christ's Preferred Method

Because this is the most effective way to win souls,
it was Christ's preferred method; and because it was
Christ's preferred method, it is the most effective way.
We are not told just how all the twelve disciples were
won to Christ, but we are told how seven of them were.
Peter, and Andrew, and James, and John, and Philip,
and Nathanael, and Matthew, were won to Christ by
individual work.[2] It is reasonable to believe that the
method which is recorded with these seven was fol-

[1] From The Sunday School Times of June 15, 1901.
[2] See pages 171, 177 of this volume.

lowed with some or all of the others. Christ proclaimed his message by preaching, as his ministers
must do to-day; but Christ won men and women to
the acceptance of his message and of himself as
Messiah and Saviour by his loving, deeply personal,
individual evangelism—conversational evangelism it
has been well called.[1]

Yet it is not surprising that the best method of soul-
winning has not yet been as widely recognized as it
deserves.

This is so in other warfare than that of Christ with his
foes. My experience in active service in the Civil War taught
me, as I am sure it taught others on both sides in that conflict,
that the thunder of artillery was likely to be most impressive,
but that the rifles of the sharpshooters brought down more
men. This was peculiarly the case in the siege life before
Charleston and before Petersburg. The shriek and the crash
of the bursting shell told in their impressiveness, especially
upon those who were least experienced; but the quiet " hum "
or the " whiz " of the rifle of the sharpshooter did execution
as ten to one, or as a hundred to one, in comparison. Yet the
artillery officer who could tell of how many rounds he had
fired in action could boast more of his service, even if he did
not know that he had ever hit anybody, than could the best
sharpshooter on the whole line. So it is with those who address individuals for Christ. Sharpshooters may bring down
more individuals with their telling single bullets, but they cannot make the impression in the surrounding atmosphere that is
made by the big guns that are heard to thunder out from the
pulpit casements every time they open fire.[2]

The superior effectiveness of this method of soul-
winning is a matter of simple observation. We can
test this ourselves, as we ask men how they were led

---

[1] A study of our Lord's other individual work will be found in
Chapter IX of this volume.

[2] Pages 171-172.

to make the actual decision for Christ. And we properly may give weight to the recorded observation of others. After half a century's retrospect Dr. Trumbull wrote:

> The more extensive and varied has been my experience, and the more I have known of the Christian labors of others, the more positive is my conviction that the winning of one soul to Christ, or of ten thousand souls to Christ, is best done by the effort of an individual with an individual, not by the proclamation of an individual to a multitude, larger or smaller, without the accompanying or following face-to-face pleading with the single soul.

> My experience came to be varied, but in every fresh phase of that experience the pre-eminent value of work for one soul at a time, over work for a multitude of souls on the same occasion, stands out as the truth beyond challenge or question. This was my conviction in the first days of my Christian consecration. This is my conviction to-day more positively than ever before. However others may feel about it, I cannot have a doubt on the subject. Winning one soul at a time usually results in the winning of a multitude of souls in the process of time. But addressing a multitude of souls, and urging them all to trust and serve Christ, may not be the means of winning even one soul to Christ, now or at any time.[1]

Its Effectiveness in Sunday-School Work

Within a few weeks of my first entering Christ's service, I most unexpectedly found myself summoned to superintend a newly organized mission Sunday-school in Hartford. In this way I was providentially started in the line of religious work that has been my chief method of Christian effort from that time to the present. In this, my first field of Christian work, I found that I could do most and best for my charge by appealing to the individual when he and I were alone together, rather than by my most effective appeals from the desk, or by my most attractive endeavors to impress the school as a whole.

[1] Pages 24-25.

Occasionally, when a boy whose conduct and influence seemed hopelessly bad was not to be reached through anything said by teacher or superintendent in the presence of others, I found that a personal talk with him near his haunts of an evening, when no one else could see us, would give me a hold on him, so that I could lead him to a better view, and a higher estimate, of his possibilities and duties. A good superintendent or a good teacher will often do more for Christ and for the most incorrigible pupil by a half-hour's talk with that pupil all by himself out of the school than is done for such a person in a year's time by superintendent and teacher in the school or class as a whole.[1]

Its Effectiveness in College

More than thirty years ago, I was present at a meeting of clergymen of different denominations, where a proposition was being considered of inviting a well-known " evangelist " to conduct a series of " revival meetings " in the community. Some of these clergymen criticized the methods of work and the manner of this evangelist. By and by a clergyman who was something of a sacramentarian in his views and practises, and therefore least likely to be in sympathy with revival methods, surprised all present by saying, earnestly:

" You will understand that the public methods of this man, in his work, are not such as I myself should incline to; but I want to bear testimony to his fidelity to his Master in all his life course. I was his fellow-student in college. I knew him well there, and I can speak understandingly of his ways. In all the four years of his college course, no student could be six weeks there without having to meet squarely the question of his personal relations to Christ, in consequence of the loving and earnest appeals of that follower of Christ. I knew more than one who was thus influenced by him. In my own case, I was a skeptic when I entered college, and I had little thought on the subject of religion anyway. But that man's appeals I had to meet, and I could not resist them. It is in consequence of his faithfulness that my life is given to the

[1] Pages 25-26.

Christian ministry. And now, whatever I think of that man's public Christian methods, I cannot but be grateful for his personal fidelity to his Master and ours." [1]

Its Effectiveness in Politics

National politics was just then assuming more importance as a great moral issue, in view of the struggle over the extension of slavery into free territory. It was about the time of the formation of the Republican party. I was on the stump for the first candidates of that party; and I was active in the work of canvassing for the election of those candidates. In this field, as in the mission Sunday-school field, I found that the effective political work was to be done, not in the public meetings, addressed by eloquent speakers, but in the quiet, systematic searching out of the individual voter, and winning him to the right side. Indeed, I had the privilege of introducing and advocating measures for an extension of this canvassing for individual voters which were novel then, but which gained in recognition and prominence as their superior effectiveness was evidenced. No political campaign is won by speakers on the stump. Stump speeches are well enough in their way. They arouse enthusiasm and make voters ready to work; but the campaign is won by the man-to-man canvass of the individual voter. One man is more than a hundred in the field of missions or of politics. Until that thought prevails, the world will never be won to Christ, or to any good cause.

Its Effectiveness in Every Field

After my return from the army I was again in the Sunday-school missionary field, which I had left to go out as a chaplain. For ten years I addressed gatherings of persons in numbers from ten or fifteen to five or six thousand each. In this work I went from Maine to California, and from Minnesota to Florida. This gave me an opportunity to test the relative value of speeches to gathered assemblies. Later, I have been for more than twenty-five years an editor of a religious

[1] Pages 153-154.

periodical that has had a circulation of more than a hundred thousand a week during much of the time. Meanwhile I have published more than thirty different volumes. Yet looking back upon my work, in all these years, I can see more direct results of good through my individual efforts with individuals, than I can know of through all my spoken words to thousands upon thousands of persons in religious assemblies, or all my written words on the pages of periodicals or of books. And in this I do not think that my experience has been wholly unlike that of many others who have had large experience in both spheres of influence.

Reaching one person at a time is the best way of reaching all the world in time. Reaching one person at a time is the best way of reaching a single individual. Therefore seeking a single individual is the best way of winning one person or a multitude to Christ. The world is made up of individuals. Christ longs for individuals to be in his service. Therefore he who considers Christ's love, or the world's needs, will think most of individuals, and will do most for individuals.[1]

Many of Christ's followers do not realize that they themselves were won by an individual word until they stop to recall what it was that finally threw the balance in favor of their open confession of Christ. Sermons, general evangelistic appeals, home-training, an impressive book, Sunday-school influence, may all prepare the way, but the matter is seldom closed without the individual word to the individual. The writer, brought up in a Christian home and Sunday-school, did not realize that this was so in his own case until comparatively recently, when he asked himself just what led to the final decision, as a boy of thirteen, to confess his Lord openly as Saviour. Then it came back to him. It was the word of a boy-playmate, a little younger than himself, who said to him one day, as

[1] Pages 27-30.

they talked together: "Father says that Jesus said that whoever would confess him before men, he would confess before the Father in heaven, and whoever denied him before men, he would deny before the Father in heaven.[1] I don't want him to deny me, and I'm going to join the church next communion Sunday." It was not, perhaps, meant as an invitation; it was only a boyish but manly statement of what he was going to do, and why he was going to do it. But the *reason* had never before been made so plain and convincing to the other boy, who went home to talk it over with his parents; and at the next opportunity those two lads stood up together in their home church to confess before men their Saviour, going out together from that service, one to be called to his Saviour only three years later, the other to thank God many years afterward for the fidelity of the boy-friend who won him to Christ.

Individual Work the Hardest Work

Individual soul-winning is not easy work. It is hard. It is the hardest work that God asks us to do for him. Before trying to reason out why, or to argue that the simple extending to a fellow-man of an invitation to share with us the richest joy of our life *ought* to be an easy thing to do, let us frankly admit that it is hard, and face that fact to begin with.

For any one who has ever tried the work knows this. Even those whose professional and only life-business is soul-saving find it difficult. Ask any minister-friend which is easier for him to do: to preach a

[1] Matthew 10: 32, 33.

sermon, or to seek an opportunity to talk alone with an individual about that one's spiritual welfare.

Many a man who is eloquent before a large congregation is dumb before a single individual. Such a man often confesses that he is not an effective worker in an "inquiry meeting." Even in a season of special religious interest he wants to turn the work of conversing with individuals over to somebody else.[1]

Bossuet, the great French preacher, said frankly as to this very matter: "It requires more faith and courage to say two words face to face with one single sinner, than from the pulpit to rebuke two or three thousand persons, ready to listen to everything, on condition of forgetting all." [2]

Men who have a national and an international fame as preachers to a multitude actually say—not only think, but say—that they cannot speak to an individual soul for Christ. In some instances these preachers speak of it as if they counted a sinner's personality too sacred to speak a word to, even to save his soul or to honor Christ. In other cases, they speak of their inability as an amiable weakness, instead of as a pitiable moral and spiritual defect, which proves them incompetent for their position and profession.[3]

Will It Grow Easy?

If it is so hard even for the trained minister, it is not to be expected that laymen will do it more easily. But if it is our greatest work, and if it is Christ's preferred method because the most effective method, have we the satisfaction and encouragement of knowing that this work will grow easy as we go on in its accomplishment? Will long-continued practise bring ease and facility?

It is to be hoped not. And judging from the experience of others we are not likely to be in danger,

---

[1] Page 8.   [2] Pages 9-10.   [3] Pages 169-170.

in this field, from the peril of easy accomplishment, which usually means loss of effectiveness.

If it "takes it out" of a man to sell goods, or write life insurance, or solicit advertising, or do anything else that means bringing another across from his position to ours, is there anything we ought to be more sharply watchful against in ourselves than slipping into a superficial "facility" in soul-winning? We not only must not expect the work to grow easy, but we must realize that if it does so, something is wrong. Anything but the "facile" man here!

Dr. Trumbull was often spoken of as being a man of exceptional "tact." He practised pretty constantly at individual soul-winning from the time when he first found his Saviour, at twenty-one, until his death more than fifty years later. People who knew him and his ways, and his life-long habit, have said of him, " Oh, it was 'second nature' to Dr. Trumbull to speak to a man about his soul. He fairly couldn't help doing it, it was so easy for him. *I* never could get *his* ease in the work." And in so saying they showed how little they knew of him or of the demands of this work upon every man.

The book on "Individual Work" was written after its author was seventy years of age. Hear what he had to say as to the "ease" which his long practise had brought him:

From nearly half a century of such practise, as I have had opportunity day by day, I can say that I have spoken with thousands upon thousands on the subject of their spiritual welfare. Yet, so far from my becoming accustomed to this matter, so that I can take hold of it as a matter of course, I find it as difficult to speak about it at the end of these years as at the beginning. Never to the present day can I speak to a single soul for Christ without being reminded by Satan that I am in danger of harming the cause by introducing it just now. If there is one thing that Satan is sensitive about, it is the danger of a Christian's harming the cause he loves by speaking of Christ to a needy soul. He [Satan] has more than once, or twice, or thrice, kept me from speaking on the subject by his sensitive pious caution, and he has tried a thousand times to do so. Therefore my experience leads me to suppose that he is urging other persons to try any method for souls except the best one.[1]

Have we not the answer here to the question which was passed over a moment ago, as to why this work is the hardest work in the world? Just because it *is* the most effective work for Christ, the Devil opposes it most bitterly, and always will while he is permitted to oppose anything good. The Devil strikes hardest and most persistently at the forces which will, if effective, hurt his cause most. He devotes his chief energies to those from whom he has most to fear; their sides he never leaves. Therefore the worker who seeks to win individuals to Christ may rest assured that he has, by entering upon that work, served notice upon the Devil for a life-and-death conflict; and that notice will be accepted by the Devil as an obligation to swerve the worker from his purpose whenever, by any subtle means in the Devil's power, this can be done. Let us write down large in our mental or real note-books the Devil's favorite argument:

His favorite argument with a believer is that just now is not a good time to speak on the subject. The lover of Christ and of souls is told that he will harm the cause he loves by introducing the theme of themes just now.[2]

This, then, is what we face when we enter upon

this work. The greatest and hardest work in the world, it will never grow easy, but it will never grow small. If it always remains the hardest, it always remains also the greatest. There is a character-challenge in continued difficulties that assures this work a quality of success to which easy work could never attain.

One who was making a study of the incidents in Dr. Trumbull's book started to group together first those cases that seemed to be complicated by some special difficulty, some factor that offered a noticeable obstacle to doing individual work in that case. He put down one incident, and another, and another, and another. And then he gave up that plan of classifying, for he found that he would have to put into that first group practically every case in the book! In the record of fifty years' work by one to whom this work was said to be " easy " because it had become " second-nature," there was scarcely a single instance that had not its own peculiar obstacle or reason for holding off!

Shall we not take encouragement by remembering this the next time we are tempted to discouragement by the peculiar difficulties that beset our path? As it was in that volume, so it will be in life. There will seldom be an opportunity free from some strong reason why we had better " do it later." But the Devil is back of the reason.

1. In what senses and passages is the verb "take alive" used in the New Testament?
2. What three facts may be asserted concerning individual work?
3. Does a minister's professional position give him any distinctive advantage for the doing of individual work? Give your reasons.
4. For what reasons would you say individual soul-winning is the greatest work in the world?
5. What was Dr. Duryea's comment on the need of a sick soul?
6. Mention any preacher's statement as to the need of individual work, or his example in its doing.
7. What striking fact in Christ's ministry shows what importance he attached to the work?
8. Why are less effective methods of Christian service likely to be heard from more than this most effective method of all?
9. Describe any striking instances of individual soul-winning you have known of personally, either in your own or in others' experiences, and apart from the cases mentioned in this book.
10. How does the principle of working with individuals apply in the Sunday-school; in college; in politics; in every field?
11. Consider carefully whether your own actual and final decision to accept Christ as your Saviour was induced by the word of an individual to you as an individual. If it was, describe the circumstances and the impression made upon you at the time.
12. Have you ever known any one who claimed that it was, as a rule, easy for him to do individual work? If so, what characteristics in his work do you notice?
13. Why is individual soul-winning likely to be hard work? Why ought it to be hard?

THE WORKER AND HIS EQUIPMENT

(For study before reading this chapter)

1. What would you say is the best equipment for successful individual soul-winning?
2. Of what should one make sure before attempt ing individual work?
3. Under what circumstances might one properly refrain from speaking to another on the subject of personal religion?
4. Are there dangers in this work? What are they?
5. Of what mistake should we be most afraid?
6. Can one who is conscious of personal defects and shortcomings properly undertake the work?
7. How is equipment best to be gained?

II

THE WORKER AND HIS EQUIPMENT

IS there any need to ask, now, who should do individual work? Can any follower of Christ accept Christ's offer of salvation for himself and refuse to pass it on? Layman or minister, Christ knows no distinctions here, makes no exceptions in his Commission to his followers. It is every layman's chief work, without which every other business and accomplishment of life counts as nothing, but added to which, ordinary or extraordinary occupations are tenfolded in value and effectiveness. It is every minister's chief work, without which pulpit and other labors are empty of life-bringing power, but added to which all his labors teem with life and love that are irresistible.

But what shall we say of equipment for the work before one dares begin, and of the danger of doing harm by making serious mistakes? Shall one hold back for fear of doing harm? What are the essentials of equipment? What brings effectiveness? Shall one wait until he has an expert knowledge of the Bible? Of theology? Power in argument? Skill in discussion?

To get a decisive answer to these questions, stop and consider what "individual work" is. It is simply a telling others of our experience of Christ's love, so that they may share it. This does not call first for an ex-

pert knowledge of the contents of the Bible, or of
theology, nor for skill in discussion and power in argument. It *does* call for unshaken, unshakable knowledge of what Jesus Christ has done for us, and for a
deeply-rooted purpose to share that knowledge with
others.

That is all. We must know Christ, and we must know
the one to whom we would make Christ attractive.
There are certain ways which are more likely than
others to win persons to us, and those ways it is the
purpose of this book to study. But we need not hold
off from the work even for this brief study. The best
way to begin is to begin; and the best time to begin is
now.

The real question is not, "Is this the best time for a
personal word for Christ?" but it is "Am I willing to improve
this time for Christ, and for a precious soul, whether it is the
best time or not?" If the Christian waits until the sinner
gives sign of a desire for help, or until the Christian thinks
that a loving word to the sinner will be most timely, he is not
likely to begin at all. The only safe rule for his guidance—if
indeed a Christian needs a specific rule as a guide—is to speak
lovingly of Christ and of Christ's love for the individual whenever one has an opportunity of choosing his subject of conversation in an interview with an individual who may be in
special need, yet who has given no special indication of it.
This seems to have been Paul's idea in his counsel to young
Timothy: "Preach the word; be instant in season, out of
season; bring to the proof, rebuke, exhort, with all long-
suffering and teaching." The most important of all themes
of converse would seem to be worthy of prominence in comparison with others.[1]

Of course, this does not mean that one is to engage
in this most subtle and vital work in a haphazard, pro-

[1] Pages 162-163.

miscuous way, without any reference to one's surroundings or acquaintanceship. Dr. Trumbull drew
the line of discrimination, as is shown in connection
with the following incident of one of his Northfield
visits.

Mr. Studd and some of his Cambridge associates came
to me, after the meeting, and asked my assistance in behalf of
one of their countrymen who was with them. He was a young
man standing high in his university. His father was eminent
in the nation. Hence the influence of the young man would be
great according as he used it for or against the right. He had,
as yet, no interest in the Christian work that had drawn to
Northfield some of his personal friends. He had come thither
because of his intimacy with some of them, but he had little
sympathy with them in their interest in what was represented
by the Northfield Conference. They had sought in vain to win
his interest in these things on the voyage over, and now they
had come for my help.

" Give us your help, Dr. Trumbull," said Mr. Studd. " It
would amply repay us for coming to America if we could only
win this man to Christ."

" My dear friends," I said, " I cannot help you. I have no
special power in winning souls. I have merely told you this
evening of my habit of speaking a word for Christ to those
whom God puts under my influence, or for whom, in some
way, he gives me a responsibility. This young man is not one
of that sort. I have merely met him here as one with you.
All I can say is that I will have your request in mind, and if
I meet him so that I have a right to speak to him I will not
fail to use the opportunity."

" Well, we shall be praying for you and him, and I trust
that God will open a way for a blessing." [1]

But see what followed, when a man who was careful to observe the requirements of ordinary courtesy
and to respect the rights of individuality was never-

[1] Pages 132-134.

theless prayerfully watchful and hopeful that God would open a way.

It was then nearly midnight. I left the Auditorium and went across the campus to the hall in which I had my room. As I went up the steps of that hall I saw a young man standing in the shadow. He stepped forward to meet me. It was the young Cambridge student of whom we had been speaking, and for whom his friends and associates were now praying. As I greeted him cordially, he said:

"Dr. Trumbull, I was over in the Auditorium and I heard your address. And now I want your help. When are you going away? When can I have a talk with you?"

"I'd gladly talk to-night with you," I said, "but I am not going away until to-morrow noon."

So it was arranged that I should meet him as I came out from the breakfast room early the next morning. Bidding him good-night, I went to my room to thank God and to pray to God. As I came from the breakfast room I found the "man greatly beloved" awaiting me. Together we sought a retired spot, under the trees, at some distance from the buildings. There we had a plain, free talk. He was entirely ready to take the step of submission to Christ, and of entering his service. As we knelt together in the open air, and sought God's blessing on the decision then made and the new life course then entered on, I felt that the incident was one of God's planning and leading to, and which surely had his blessing.

I was glad to report to those who had sought my help this sequel to their request of the evening before. And when I left them all, that noon, I was confident that the new disciple would be lovingly and faithfully cared for and aided in the subsequent days at Northfield and when all returned to their English homes. Some weeks later I had a letter from that young man, speaking most gratefully of that interview under the trees on that morning in Northfield—that "heaven on earth," as he called it, and as any place where God is can fairly be called. God is always better than we anticipate, if we are ready to work for souls in his behalf.[1]

[1] Pages 134-136.

A prominent preacher once sent to Dr. Trumbull, for publication in The Sunday School Times, an article on " The Dangers of Personal Evangelism." It was returned to its author unpublished. For Dr. Trumbull had learned early in his work that there is only one mistake to be really afraid of here. Of a certain experience he wrote:

> That experience with my first young convert in the army encouraged me in my individual work with individuals there. I saw that it were better to make a mistake in one's first effort at a personal religious conversation, and correct that mistake afterwards, than not to make any effort. There can be no mistake so bad, in working for an individual soul for Christ, as the fatal mistake of not making any honest endeavor. How many persons refrain from doing anything lest they should possibly do the wrong thing just now! Not doing is the worst of doing. "Inasmuch as ye did it not, depart from me," is a foretold sentence of the Judge of all.[1]

The army experience in which he at first feared he had done harm was the following:

> My first experience under fire was on a winter Sunday in Eastern North Carolina. We had bivouacked for the night in an open field, when starting on a raid into the enemy's country. As we rose in the early morning to make ready for a march, the blazing camp-fires on every side, throwing their lurid light on the stacked arms, and the moving soldiers, with the hum of conflicting voices, made a weird and impressive scene; and as I heard for the first time the command, to a company near where I stood, "Load at will," followed by the ring of the rammers in the steel rifle barrels driving home the cartridges, I was thrilled by the sounds as never before. Realizing, as I did, that when those rifles were discharged it would be in deadly conflict, and that before the day should close some

[1] Pages 76 77.

of the brave men near me would probably be in the presence of their Maker, I had a sense of responsibility for souls as never before, yet as often afterwards.

Moving about among the fire-lit groups, and looking for a man standing by himself, I came upon a soldier, a bright Connecticut boy, with whom I had often spoken in camp. He was arranging his belt at the moment. I spoke to him cheerily of the activities of the hour, and of the possibilities of the coming day. Then I asked him tenderly if he had committed himself trustfully to his Saviour.

"Ah, Chaplain! This is no time to think of such things. It would unfit me for a fight if I got to thinking about myself just now."

"It is always a time, Sergeant, for thinking about Him who is able to care for us in every hour of life or of death, and who loves us more than we can ever love him. But if you don't want to talk about this now I shall come to you when we are back in camp, if we get there together once more; and then, certainly, I can have a good talk with you about this matter, for I want you to do your duty."

Our raid was a successful one, and soon we were back in camp once more. I looked up my young sergeant friend, and told him that I had come to renew our conversation of the morning after our first night's bivouac, on the recent raid. I had a plain, earnest talk with him. He promised to go, in need and trust, to his Saviour, and commit himself to him for life and death. After a while, when we were in St. Augustine, we organized a regimental church, and this young sergeant was the first one to stand up and make a confession of his Saviour, in the presence of his regimental comrades and others. Later he connected himself with his home church in Connecticut, on my certificate of his confession of faith while in army life in the South.[1]

After a meeting at which the writer had been urging the duty of being willing to risk mistakes rather than make the greatest mistake of saying nothing for Christ, a woman present told of her experience. She

[1] Pages 73-76.

had longed to lead to Christ a girl in her Sunday-school class. One day she called upon the girl, determined to have a loving talk about the matter. But her courage failed; she talked about every subject but the greatest one, and when she left, the purpose of her call had not been mentioned. She started home in discouragement; wheeled around; went back to the house; and in a blundering, faltering way she told her young friend how she wished she would give herself to the Saviour. Then the teacher left the house for the second time and went home, but not before the girl had plainly shown that she was very angry at her caller for what she had dared to do. At the next communion service of the church that young girl stood up and, confessing Christ as her Saviour, was received into full membership in the church. Her teacher went to her with a full heart, told her how glad she was, and asked her what it was that had led her to take the step. "Why, it was what you said to me that day you called," was the reply. And one Sunday-school teacher was rejoiced that she had dared to make a "mistake."

Our Feelings and Our Defects

Our "feelings" have no place as a factor in this work. What is called "the passion for souls" would seem to be a feeling of overwhelming desire to win others to Christ that very few possess or ever will possess. But that absence of feeling neither relieves us of our simple duty nor need hinder us in its doing. We do not have to like one before seeking to win him to Christ. If we saw a neighbor's house on fire, we should not stop to weigh our feelings for that neighbor before sounding the alarm. Feelings will seldom lead

one to the doing of this supreme duty. But both love
and liking for a fellow-man are very likely to follow
our unselfish efforts to bring this greatest of blessings
to him. Our constant effort in the Christian life ought
to be to get the better of our feelings, and not to let our
feelings get the better of us.

What of the worker's own character, or lack of
character, as bearing on the doing of this work?
Shall we let the consciousness of our own unworthiness, our many shortcomings, keep us from it? Shall
we hold off until our own lives are more nearly in accord with the Christ-life, better examples of what
Christ can do for one?

Why should we? Is not our own unworthiness,
after all, one of the chief appeals that we can make to
those who are like us in this terrible need of a Saviour?
We speak as *saved sinners,* not as superior beings.
We *know* whereof we speak, for we know the need,
and we know how great is the saving love that can
outweigh even our unworthiness. That love of Christ
we would share, for all need it even as we do. "For
we preach not ourselves, but Christ Jesus as Lord,
and ourselves as your servants for Jesus' sake.... But
we have this treasure in earthen vessels, that the ex-
ceeding greatness of the power may be of God, and
not from ourselves." [1]

It is not so much a question of our defects, as of
Christ's sufficiency, nor of the difficulty in the way of
speaking, as of our purpose to overcome such difficulty. A pathetically striking instance of insistent and
joyous determination to speak for Christ to individuals is given in S. H. Hadley's account of Jerry

[1] 2 Corinthians 4: 5, 7.

McAuley's first efforts. While in prison Jerry had been won to his Saviour.

He immediately went to work with an ardor and courage that would put many of us missionaries to shame. Under the rules of the prison at that time, very little opportunity was given to speak to any one. Only as they were marching to and fro, with lockstep, from prison to workshop, from workshop to meals, and then back to prison again, could he speak to the man in front and the one behind, telling the burning news that was filling his soul, that he had found Jesus, that his sins were pardoned, and how happy he was in his new-found joy.

At the table he was able to speak to the one on his right hand, and the one on his left, but even with this limited opportunity a wonderful revival broke out in the prison as a result of Jerry's labors. Missionaries of the city went up, and every opportunity was given them by the management. Bible classes were formed of the converts, and wonderful work was done for God. Jerry was the center of all this activity.[1]

Of this we may be sure: nothing brings into one's own life such a powerful lift to higher levels as the doing of individual work for others. It is bound to raise one's own standards of life and conduct. It is the most effective safeguard against personal failure that we can ever find. The best way to conquer self is to forget self in an effort to help "the other fellow."

Not only will continued work in this field strengthen our spiritual fiber and deepen our spiritual life, but it will inevitably lead us into more thoughtful and profitable Bible study, broaden our other interests, increase our sensitiveness and tact, and give us ever greater power to love. Yet all these blessings to self will come only from a complete forgetting of self in our loving interest in others.

[1] S. H. Hadley's "Down in Water Street," pages 23-24.

Our Right to be Confident

Finally, as to the confidence with which we enter upon this work. If it is the greatest work to which God calls us every one, can we be in any doubt as to its having his blessing? There is no room here for self-confidence; but there is no room, either, for lack of God-confidence. We have the same Power working with us that Jesus had with him. "As the Father hath sent me," he says to his disciples, " even so send I you."[1] Results we shall not always see. But results we must always hope for and believe in. "You don't expect to have conversions every time you preach, do you?" Spurgeon is said to have asked a young minister who was seeking how to get greater results from his ministry. "Oh, no," said the young man. "Then you won't," was the retort.

Topics and Questions for Study and Discussion

(To test one's grasp of the contents of the chapter)

1. Why are none exempt from the obligation to do individual soul-winning?
2. What effect has the doing of this work upon one's other occupations?
3. What is individual work, simply defined?
4. What is not called for, in the way of equipment? What is called for?
5. What two persons must we know in order to do the work well?
6. How would you draw the line between haphazard, promiscuous working, and that which is not?

[1] John 20: 21.

7. What is the only mistake that need really be feared?
8. Have you ever known personally of an instance where the worker feared that a mistake had been made, yet which resulted well? Describe it.
9. What place have our feelings in this work? Why?
10. Should a person who is conscious of failures in his own life attempt this work? Why?
11. What is the effect of this work upon oneself?
12. Give two strong reasons why we should have confidence as we enter upon the work.

NEED OF A LIFE-RESOLVE

Preparatory Thoughts and Questions

(For study before reading this chapter)

1. What do you think, in general, of the wisdom of making pledges, or resolutions?
2. Has any one a right to expect Christ to pledge Himself to save him, who is unwilling to pledge himself, in turn, to serve Christ faithfully? Is this a fair way to look at the pledge question?
3. What statement did you make or give assent to when you united with the church (this can be obtained from your pastor)? Study this, and ascertain its bearing on your obligation to do individual work. Is it equivalent to a pledge to do this work?
4. Frame a simple form of pledge or resolution to make a practise of individual soul-winning.
5. What gain would there be in the definite, prayerful making of such a resolution?

III

NEED OF A LIFE–RESOLVE

H ENRY Clay Trumbull was brought up in a home
where exceptionally high standards prevailed,
where both parents were earnest Christians, and where
every influence tended Christward. Yet, as is so often
the case in similar surroundings, he passed through
boyhood and out of his teens without having made any
definite confession of Christ as his Saviour.

He left his home in Stonington, Connecticut, to
take a clerkship in a Hartford railroad office. About
that time there was a season of religious revival, both
in Stonington and Hartford, with special meetings in
the latter city under the leadership of the famous
evangelist Finney.

But as I was boarding at a house where the young men
at the table had only words of contempt or ridicule for the
whole matter, I attended none of the meetings, did not at the
first hear Mr. Finney, and had no conscious interest in his
work or its results.[1]

Before he left Stonington, one of his most intimate
friends there had taken the stand for Christ, and so
had others. But no one had a word to say on the
subject to young Trumbull.

Had any one of them, or had any one else, spoken a per-

[1] Page 12.

sonal word to me on the subject, at that time, I would have welcomed it gladly; but no such word came.

I was, indeed, somewhat surprised that my friend had no word to say on the subject, then or at some time later, intimate as he and I were. Especially was this the case as we corresponded freely during his college course in Yale. When I was about twenty-one years old I removed to Hartford, and I continued to correspond freely with my Stonington friend.[1]

What followed came, therefore, with the more unexpectedness.

One noon, as I was returning from my mid-day meal, I stopped at the post-office for the noon mail. A letter came from my Stonington friend. This surprised me, for I had not yet acknowledged his letter of a few days before. As I read the first few lines of the letter, I saw that it was a personal appeal to me. At once crumpling the letter in my hand I thrust it into my pocket, saying to a friend who was with me, "I think there must be a big revival in Stonington, if it has set my old friend preaching to me." Then, brushing the subject away from my mind, I started down Asylum Street toward my office and my work.

But the subject of that letter, and the letter itself, would not stay brushed away. I asked myself how it was that that letter, on that subject, had been written. In all our years of intimacy since my friend had come out openly for Christ, he had never before said or written a word on this subject. Had it been an easy thing for him to do now? Was it a desire for his own enjoyment, or a desire for my good, that had prompted this writing? It was worth while to read that letter, and consider its contents, before throwing it aside permanently. These were the thoughts that naturally ran in my mind as I walked toward my office.

The office of the chief engineer, where my work lay, was on the third floor of one of the stone towers of the railroad station. Instead of stopping in that office, where I usually stopped, I passed through it, and went into a little map-closet

[1] Pages 11-12.

on that upper floor. Shutting myself into the map-closet, where I could be entirely alone, I took out from my pocket the crumpled letter, smoothed it out, and began with real interest to read.[1]

The letter was an earnest appeal from one man, who had found the Saviour, to another who did not yet know that joy. It opened with a half-apology for the seeming " intrusion; " went on to explain how hard it had been to write on this subject; added " I may never have the courage to address you again in this manner;" and closed with the earnest hope that the reader would therefore " be advised by me now." What a timorous, reluctant effort it was, yet how blessed!

Before I had read the last of this letter, I was on my knees in that corner map-room in that lofty tower summit, asking forgiveness of God, and committing myself to a long slighted Saviour. That was a turning-point in my life course; and in a half-century that has passed since then I have been renewedly more and more grateful for the writing of that letter, and for the loving spirit that prompted it. And I have wished that other friends were as true to their friends.[1]

The lesson of the need of individual effort for souls was just beginning to take root in this man's life, as it was the start of his own new life. But see with what startling vigor the lesson was reinforced!

So soon as I had come to the point of Christian decision for myself, I looked about me for another man. I did not have far to go. An associate with me in the office of the chief engineer was a fellow-boarder with me in the house which was my temporary home. We were accustomed to walk together to and from the boarding-house and the office. We were near each other all day in the office, and we sat near each other at the

boarding-house table. As we walked together from the house
to the office, I told my friend of my new decision for Christ,
and I urged him to make a like decision.

Here was the answer that burned in the lesson so
deep:

"Trumbull, your words cut me to the heart. You little
think how they rebuke me. I've long been a professed follower
of Christ; and you have never suspected this, although we've
been in close association in house and office for years. I've
never said a word to you for the Saviour whom I trust. I've
never urged you to trust him. I've never said a word for him.
And now a follower of his, and a friend of yours, from a distance, has been the means of leading you to him. And here
are you, inviting me to come to that Saviour of whom I have
been a silent follower for years. May God forgive me for my
lack of faithfulness!" [1]

Is it surprising that those two incidents in Christian
work, one bringing him into eternal life, the other
revealing the careless neglect of the greatest matter in
the world so common among Christian people, had
an effect on this man that he determined, God helping
him, he would never outgrow? The effect was deliberately crystallized in this way:

Then it was that I made a purpose and resolve for life.
The purpose I formed was, as an imperative duty, not to fail
in my Christian life in the particular way that these two
friends of mine confessed that they had consciously failed. I
determined that as I loved Christ, and as Christ loved souls,
I would press Christ on the individual soul, so that none who
were in the proper sphere of my individual responsibility or
influence should lack the opportunity of meeting the question
whether or not they would individually trust and follow
Christ. The resolve I made was, that whenever I was in such
intimacy with a soul as to be justified in choosing my subject

,of conversation, the theme of themes should have prominence between us, so that I might learn his need, and, if possible, meet it.[1]

There was the life-resolve that shaped and controlled that life during the more than fifty years that followed its prayerful making. That the efforts in individual soul-winning which were the direct result of the resolve were in every sense the richest and most blessed part of that long lifetime of varied service, Dr. Trumbull himself never doubted, nor do others who have had opportunity to review his life. Is it a resolve that any disciple of Christ ought to hesitate to make? Is to do so anything more than the meeting of our simplest duty as Christ's loyal followers? But could anything bring a greater blessing, a richer harvest of souls, into the Kingdom to-day, than the making and keeping of this resolve by Christian people generally? Let us think of this. Here is the resolution that we are facing:

> Whenever I am justified in choosing my subject of conversation with another, the theme of themes shall have prominence between us, so that I may learn his need, and, if possible, meet it.

Topics and Questions for Study and Discussion

(To test one's grasp of the contents of the chapter)

1. Why does it not necessarily follow that the influences of a Christian home, and of church and Sunday-school training, always result in one's accepting Christ as Saviour?

[1] Page 23.

2. What is a common cause of surprise to those who are not Christians, in the attitude of their Christian friends?

3. Why is it that a large number of people in any community are always unreached by revival meetings?

4. How may revival meetings be given greatest effectiveness?

5. What incident made a profound impression on H. Clay Trumbull just after he had been won to Christ by an individual appeal?

6. Do you think that that experience, in his first attempt at soul-winning, might be duplicated in a good many cases to-day, or not?

7. What was the life-resolve that the young convert made?

8. Analyze that resolve, showing how it guards against haphazard or discourteous effort, under what circumstances it calls for the doing of the work, why the resolve ought to be made, and what is its definite and declared purpose.

WINNING AT THE START

PREPARATORY THOUGHTS AND QUESTIONS

(For study before reading this chapter)

1. State the ultimate purpose of the work in which we are seeking to gain proficiency.
2. Why, should you say, does much depend upon the way in which we approach a person?
3. What should we try to accomplish in our approach?
4. What is the best kind of approach to make?
5. What is the worst kind of approach to make?
6. Give your own definition of tact.
7. What place has tact in this work? Why?
8. Was Jesus tactful? Can you give any illustrations of his tact?
9. What place has personal criticism in this work?
10. Mention two or three sure ways to win people to us.

IV

WINNING AT THE START

WHEN we are face to face with an opportunity, which means face to face with one whom we would win to Christ, how shall we begin? *What shall we be thinking most about as we prepare to come into close quarters?* Shall we be hunting in our memory for a Bible text to quote? Shall we be running over in our mental note-book the various groups or classifications of "cases," so that we may decide in which pigeon-hole this "case" belongs? Shall we try to remember how this or that noted soul-winner worked?

If we concentrate on any of these lines at the moment of beginning, we shall be missing the most important factor in the situation. When a man is fishing with rod and line and fly, and is about to cast, what holds his chief attention then, and from then on? It is the *fish,* is it not? When a man is after game in the woods, and is about to attempt to bring his game down, what is the one thing in the world on which his eyes and thoughts and interests are riveted? *The game itself.* He must forget everything else in an absorbed, alert watching of the animal and its every movement. He must *know* his game, and its interests, if he would capture it.

If we would take a man alive for Christ, we must first of all know something, be it ever so little, about that man and his present interests. Our knowledge may be gained in ten seconds; again, it may take ten months to gain. But we can never have this needed knowledge of the man, as a first step toward winning the man himself, unless we devote our whole energy, for the time being, to knowing the man. Therefore it is that *he* must fill our whole horizon as we prepare to come into close quarters with him. We must be thinking not about *others,* but about *this other;* just this one in the whole universe.

This is the simple secret of " tact,"—that mysterious power which a few favored ones seem to possess, and which, if one does not happen to have the " gift," is regretfully supposed to be beyond one's reach. But "tact" is simply " touch": a touch on the right spot rather than the wrong; a touch which will win another, rather than antagonize him; a touch in keeping with, rather than opposed to, his present interests. And it is impossible to touch one at a point that will interest him unless we know something of what his interests are. The art of taking men alive calls for tact at the very beginning, which means, first of all, studying your man.

This concentrating all our attention on the individual at the outset, so that we may know what interests him, is to enable us to put forward something that shall attract and hold his attention. In fishing, the attractive thing thus put forward by the fisherman is called bait. And bait is a prime essential in the man-fishing to which Christ called his disciples, and in which he promised to train them to expertness.

For let us bear in mind that we are in the business of *winning* men to Christ. We cannot win by antagonizing. And we must win by drawing men to *us,* as a first step in drawing them to Christ.

The Other Man's Interests as Bait

It is the other man's interests just where they are, and as they are, not as we think or know they ought to be, that we must recognize and work with. We cannot expect others to cross over from their interests to ours until we have first crossed over from our interests to theirs.

The Master Fisherman has given us a striking instance of the use of this bait-principle, in the record of the training of some of his first disciples.

He had the whole world to choose from, when he began the special training of the few men with whom he was to entrust the continuance of the winning of the world to himself. Several of these chosen few were fishermen. That was not an accident, nor was their fishing a mere incident in their previous life. The principles of successful fishing were already dominant factors in their lives. And one of their earliest lessons in soul-winning was taught through a miraculous fishing experience that Jesus gave them. Still more clearly there was no accident in this. Our study of Christ's methods of winning men to himself, and our study of what one of his followers was permitted to do in the same work, reveal something of why Christ chose fishermen to be his apostles, and how he trained fishermen to become fishers of men.

Even the Son of God did not take it for granted that men would be interested in him or his message until he had first interested himself in them. Shall we expect to do better than he? If not, we must be willing to work as he did. Let us watch him at work on the lakeside.[1]

He is teaching the eager multitude the word of God. But, always more interested in the individual than in the crowd, he is watching some fishermen near by whom he knows and whom he has been trying to awaken to a sense of his mission, and to the need of taking part in it. So he asks one of them to help by permitting the use of his boat as a pulpit; and then he goes on with his message to the multitude.

With what indication of response or interest from the fishermen? None at all. The reason is plain enough. They had had a profitless, exhausting night of it in their trade. A fisherman does not mind getting tired out by hard work if he has a boat-load of fish to show for his efforts. But to work all night and take nothing! The physical exhaustion then is doubled by the discouragement. And the nets have to be cleaned, too, just as though the catch had been a big one! Washing nets, at its best, is pretty dull business; but washing nets that have stayed empty all night is enough to take the heart out of any man.

It was a cheerless, discouraging day that was just breaking for those tired men by the sea. What if a great teacher *was* expounding precious spiritual truth within earshot? Human nature wanted none of that— just then. Could any human being fairly have been expected to be interested in spiritual matters under those circumstances?

Jesus knew how it was. It did not call for his supernatural insight into " what was in man " to appreciate that the men he was trying to train were more

<hr>

[1] Luke 5: 1-11.

interested in the fish they had failed to catch, that morning, than in anything else in the universe.

Yet this fact, instead of making him impatient, or deterring him from any attempt to go on with their training, was to him a challenge, an invitation. It was his opportunity to use tact, to use bait. He must touch them at the point of their present interests, unworthy though these interests might seem in comparison with higher spiritual matters. He must use a bait that would attract these men just as they were, without waiting until they should come, of their own accord, to worthier interests.

Fish—the fish they hadn't caught—were their present interest. Fish, then, must be the bait. So his first word to them is, " Put out into the deep, and let down your nets for a draught." They remonstrated, of course.

But because his very manner showed them that he was intent on giving their own temporal interests his supreme attention, they yielded. And then, after he had given them such proof of his genuine interest in them as they never forgot, and they had taken care of the nets that were breaking and the boats that were sinking from the draught of fishes which *he* had helped them to catch, they were ready to think of other things than fish. They were ready, then, to be interested in *anything* that Jesus had to offer, because he had first interested himself in them.

Now, and not until now, can Christ hope for a response as he says, in effect: " I have helped you to catch fish; I want you to help me to catch men. From henceforth thou shalt take men alive."

It is so easy to miss the principles of Christ's meth-

ods of soul-winning if we will not look for them. One
of the most prominent commentators of this generation
has actually written, of this incident: " There was absolutely no purpose, either of demonstration of Christ's
mission or of help to human needs, to be served by the
miracle. Its only significance is symbolical." But is it,
indeed, either necessary or reasonable to suppose that
the Master turned aside from his spiritual teaching and
caused the miraculous draught of fishes simply in order
that he might have a good illustration of what he
wanted these disciples to take up as their life-work?
They were already fishermen; he could easily have
said to them, with their nets empty, " from henceforth
thou shalt take men alive," and they would have understood him. But the empty nets would effectually have
killed their interest in the invitation.

They were not interested in taking men alive then;
they were absorbingly interested in catching fish. To
be sure, this was not nearly so worthy an interest as
the saving of men's souls; but Christ took men as they
were, not as he would have liked them to be.

How differently most of us would have handled
that situation! How we should have stormed and
protested and argued with those men, indignantly
urging them to forget their fish for a few minutes and
turn their attention to something worth while! How
surprised or hurt or discouraged we have been, in our
own experiences, because those upon whom we have
urged the blessings of life in Christ are obviously and
persistently more interested in the unworthy affairs of
this unworthy world! Have we ever given ourselves
in any absorbing way to a study of what we are pleased
to consider their " unworthy " interests, in order to be

of genuine service to them? If we have not, we are failing in a first principle of the art upon which depends our success in the Great Commission.

The Bait of Honest Commendation

We cannot do to-day just as Christ did by the lake-side,—work a miracle to win men's interest. But there is another kind of bait that is within the reach of us all, and that calls for no miracle to use. It is a bait that Jesus himself used freely in his soul-winning.[1] This is the bait of *honest commendation.* It will land the most slippery human fish alive. No man can resist it. A word, heartily spoken, of sincere commendation for a fellow-being, will disarm opposition and draw him to us more effectively than any other method. It is the best human bait in the world.

Perhaps one reason why honest commendation is so effective in challenging a person's interest is because it is so rare. A friend of the writer's, passing through a town on his travels, saw an old gray-haired colored man hard at work in the roadway. He greeted the toiler pleasantly:

"Uncle, that's a good piece of work you're doing."

The old man stopped, straightened up, looked the other over, then said slowly:

"Say, boss, you doan live in this town, do you?"

"No, why?" asked the visitor.

"I been workin' hyar twenty years, and yo' the fust man ever told me anything like that." Which was probably sober fact.

"But," says some one, "that's all well enough with a person whom you *can* commend, but suppose

---

[1] See Chapter IX, pages 176-178, of this volume.

you are working with one whom you can *not* commend?" Wait a moment! Say that again! "One
whom you can not commend?" That person does not
live. If we think that we have ever met such a one,
the fault is with ourselves, not with the seemingly
unlovely person. This truth is brought out in the
further study of Christ's methods,[1] and it will become
plainer as we go on in our other studies in this series.

Commending a Whiskey-Drinker

An illustration of the possibility and the gain of
using honest commendation at the outset with one
whose confidence we would win, is found in a railroad train experience resulting from such an opportunity as might come to any traveler.

Entering, one November morning, at the Grand Central
Station in New York, a crowded train for Boston, I found the
only vacant seat was one alongside of a pleasant-faced, florid-
complexioned, large-framed young man, and that seat I took,
and began to read the morning paper. After a few minutes my
seat-mate took from his valise a large case bottle of whiskey
and a metal drinking-cup. Before drinking himself, he proffered it to me. As I thanked him and declined it, he drank
by himself.[2]

Not a particularly hopeful outlook for soul-winning, most of us would feel, and still less did there
seem to be any chance for the bait of commendation.
But the fisherman was doing all that he could do as
yet, by studying his man and holding himself in readi-
ness.

I still read my paper, but I thought of my seat-mate, and
I watched for an opportunity. In a little while he again turned

---

[1] In Chapter IX of this volume.   [2] Pages 31-32.

to his valise, and, as before, took out his whiskey bottle. Once more he offered it to me, and again I declined it with thanks. As he put away the bottle, after drinking from it the second time, he said:

"Don't you ever drink, my friend?"

"No, my friend, I do not."

"Well, I guess you think I'm a pretty rough fellow." [1]

Perhaps some of us, if we had felt any responsibility at all for speaking a word for Christ to this seat-mate, would have already pointed out the danger and the wrong of his drinking. Or if not, we might have felt that he himself had now made the opening for a word of honest reproof, and with that we would have begun. Surely there was no opportunity to commend anything in this whiskey-drinking stranger. But Dr. Trumbull had learned the first principle of man-fishing, and here was his friendly, honest answer, based on the one admirable quality in this man that loving penetration had discovered:

"I think you're a very generous-hearted fellow."

And then a frank suggestion could be made in the same instant, because the first word had won, not repelled, the man. Even now it must be made in a way that should not repel by giving offense, so he continued:

"But I tell you frankly I don't think your whiskey-drinking is the best thing about you."

Nor did the whiskey-drinker ever live who was in any doubt on this point, and promptly came the answer:

"Well, I don't believe it is."

[1] Page 32.

"Why do you keep it up, then?" was the friendly question.

And from that skilful, loving, winning start it was not difficult to have an earnest talk with this young fellow.

At this he told me something of his story. He was a Massachusetts country boy, now a clerk in a large New York jobbing house. He was just going to his old country home to spend Thanksgiving. He confessed that he had fallen into bad ways in the city, very different ways from those of his boyhood in Massachusetts. I asked him about his mother, and he spoke lovingly and tenderly of her. He said he knew she was praying for him constantly. This brought us into close quarters. I told him that I was sure his mother would be happy if he prayed for himself, and that he knew that he ought to do this. I urged him to do it.

He was evidently surprised and touched by my expressions of interest in him. Then he spoke gratefully of another show of interest in him. He said:

"I was coming up Broadway, the other night. It was about midnight. I had been having 'a time.' I'll own up, I'd been off on a regular 'bum.' A little ahead of me I saw a fellow in a doorway, and he came out as if he were coming for me. I squared away towards him, as I came near him, for I thought he was 'laying' for me. But as I got opposite to him he just gave me a card, and asked me to accept it, and I passed on.

"When I got to the next lamp-post I looked at that card, and it told about a place on Twenty-third Street, called a 'Young Men's Christian Association,' where they'd like to have young men come in any time, and make themselves at home. And there that fellow, that I'd squared away to, was out there at midnight 'laying' for just such 'bummers' as I was, to invite 'em to come in and make themselves at home in that place. I 'swow,' I mean to go up to that place, when I get back, and give 'em five dollars for the good they're doing."

I told my seat-mate that those who love Christ love such as he, because Christ loves them. And I urged him to make his Thanksgiving Day at his old homestead a real day of

thanksgiving, by telling his good mother that her prayers for
him were answered.

"That would make my old mother pretty happy, if I did
that," he said heartily.

"Wouldn't you like to make your old mother happy, as
you go home to have a Thanksgiving with her?" I asked.

"Indeed I would," he said.

As we came to my Hartford home, where I was to leave
the train, I took his hand and urged him again to do what he
knew was his duty, and which would gladden his good mother's
heart. He thanked me for my interest in his welfare. He
promised to talk with his mother of our conversation. He
assured me that he would endeavor to profit by our talk. I
urged him to commit himself to Christ as the all-sufficient
Saviour, and we parted.[1]

What shall we say of denouncing another's specific
sin, or criticizing for some shortcoming or fault?
Would that be a good way to begin? Would it have
been so in the case of the whiskey-drinking seat-mate?
Is criticism or denunciation likely to draw two people
close together? There is grave doubt whether it ever
does. It certainly has no place in the work of individual soul-*winning*. Christ himself did not use it
in that work. The instances where he did use it are
considered later.[2] Let us bear ever in mind that the
first principle of this work is the drawing of men to
us, not the driving of men away. Fishermen do not
thrash the water or throw stones at the fish when they
begin.

Praising a Profane Sea-Captain

Another illustration of the bait-principle of commendation, showing the importance of first winning

a man to ourselves if we would later win him to Christ, and illustrating the skill by which honest commendation may be made effective, is found in a wartime experience of the chaplain's.

> Army-transport life gave many an opportunity of personal work with souls, as well as did public preaching. Along the Atlantic coast the Civil War demanded frequent and varied use of transports. At one time in North Carolina our division made a raid into the interior of the state, cutting itself off from its base of supplies, and exposing itself to capture by a force of the enemy in its rear. It seemed, both to us and to the enemy, that we were hopelessly hemmed in; but, at the close of the day in which we had accomplished the main object of our raid, we turned directly toward a river, and on reaching its banks found a number of small vessels waiting there to receive us, in accordance with the plan of our commanding general. These transports had been brought up to this point so that we might board them, and quietly slip down the stream during the night, thus flanking the force that had come into our rear.
>
> Boarding those vessels and getting under way was an exciting movement. If the enemy discovered our position in season to attack us before we were fairly started, there was little hope of escape for us. The skipper of the craft on which our regiment embarked was a character. He felt the responsibilities of the hour, and he gave evidence of this in his superabundant profanity accompanying every order which he issued. I had never heard such abounding and varied oaths as he poured out in the half-hour from the time we began to come on board till we were fairly afloat and were moving down the stream. Of course, then was no time to begin preaching to him.[1]

That was where ordinary common sense needed to be used, and was. If the chaplain had attempted a word of personal appeal just then, the chaplain might have gone overboard. But he was none the less measuring the man, and preparing.

I could merely watch and study him. But that I did, with real interest.

When, at last, all was quiet, and the evening had come on, and the old skipper was evidently gratified with the success of the movement so far, I accosted him with complimentary words as to the skill and energy he had shown in his command.[1]

The bait was cast. But suppose, instead, that the chaplain, even now in the quiet of the evening, had commenced his conversation with an expression of regret at the skipper's profanity, and had called his attention to the bad example he was setting, and the harmful influence he must be exerting among the other men, if he did not reform. How much farther, and with what profit, do you think that conversation would have gone? The bait of commendation, on the other hand, was readily taken, as it always is.

This opened up a conversation, in the course of which he told of other exciting experiences he had had in other parts of the world. I listened attentively, and he saw that I was appreciative and sympathetic.

To be a good listener is one of the surest ways of winning and holding men. The " I can help you " attitude is fatal in this work; the "you are helping, or interesting, me " spirit is one of the secrets of success.

Presently he spoke of a particularly perilous time he once had on the coast of Africa.

"Ah, Captain! I suppose you had charge of a slaver then," I said.

Seeing that he had "given himself away," he replied, with a quiet chuckle:

[1] Pages 82 83.

"Yes, Chaplain, I've been up to purty nigh ev'rythin', in my time, 'cept piety."[1]

Is it not remarkable how sure the "opening" is to come when we are looking and praying and planning for it?

"Well, Captain," I responded, "wouldn't it be worth your while to try your hand at that also before you die, so as to make the whole round?"

"Well, I suppose that would be fair, Chaplain."

The way was now open for a free and kindly talk. As we stood together there, on the vessel's deck, going down the stream by night, we talked pleasantly and earnestly, and I got at the early memories of his boyhood life in New England. Then I knew I was near his heart.[2]

There might not have seemed to be much in common, a few hours earlier, between the young Connecticut chaplain and the weather-beaten, profane sea-captain. But that the younger man had already succeeded in winning the other to himself personally, as a powerful aid in winning him later to Christ, comes out in what happened that first night.

By and by, all of us made ready for the night. There was but one berth in the cabin. That was the captain's. Our officers were to sleep on the cabin floor. The captain said to me:

"Chaplain, you turn in in my stateroom. There's a good berth there."

"No, no, thank you, Captain," I said. "Let the Colonel take that."

"It isn't the Colonel's room; it's mine, and I want *you* to take it."

"It would never do," I said, "for the Colonel to sleep on the floor while I slept in a berth. But I thank you just as much for your kindness, Captain."

I lay down with the other officers on the cabin floor. While I was asleep I felt myself being rolled around, and I found that the captain had pulled his mattress out of his berth, and laid it on the floor, and he was now rolling me on to it. I appreciated the gruff kindness of the old slaver-skipper, and my heart was drawn the closer to this new parishioner of mine. Nor did I lose my hold on him when we were fairly at New Berne, at the close of this trip. I was again with him in the waters of South Carolina, and he came again and again to our regimental chapel-tent on St. Helena Island to attend religious services there. I saw that I had a hold on him.[1]

The most hopeful indication we can ever have in this work comes when one whom we would win shows an interest in the spiritual welfare of another. How the chaplain's heart must have been gladdened at this sign from his skipper-parishioner!

One week-day he called at my tent, having a brother skipper with him, whom he introduced to me, and then fell back, leaving us together. He joined my tent-mate, the adjutant, and stood watching while I talked with the new comer. He told the adjutant, with a string of oaths, that his foolish friend didn't believe there was a God, so he'd "brought him over here for the chaplain to tackle." It was fresh evidence that life was stirring in him, and that therefore he wanted another saved.[2]

Did it pay, to begin by seeking and finding something to commend, honestly and heartily, in a cursing old sea-captain, and then to hold lovingly to him in the effort to show him his real Captain? See the end:

When the war was over, I heard of that slaver-skipper in his New England seaport home. At more than threescore years of age he had come as a little child to be a disciple of Jesus; he had connected himself with the church, and was living a consistent Christian life. He was honestly trying his

hand at "piety" before he died, and so was completing the
round of life's occupation. For this I was glad.[1]

Topics and Questions for Study and Discussion

(To test one's grasp of the contents of the chapter)

1. What shall we think most about as we prepare to speak
   with some one on the subject of his relation to Christ?
2. What is "tact"?
3. What is the immediate purpose of our seeking to know
   the man and his interests?
4. Name two kinds of bait that are effective in man-fishing.
5. By what method, using which kind of bait, did Jesus
   win certain disciples to the work of his Kingdom?
6. Have you ever known any one whose interests were all
   and wholly unworthy? Have you ever been surprised
   to discover worthy interests in one in whom you had
   supposed they were lacking? Describe the case.
7. When a person's chief interests are wholly removed
   from, or even antagonistic to, Christ's interests, how
   can you go about helping him?
8. Have you ever tried winning an indifferent or an un-
   friendly person by commendation? Describe the case.
9. What was the critical point in the conversation with
   the young whiskey-drinker in the railroad train?
10. What is the chief objection to criticism or denunciation
    in this work?
11. What was apparently the single possibility of commenda-
    tion in the whiskey-drinker? In the profane sea-cap-
    tain?
12. What attitude is fatal in this work? What attitude is
    sure to draw people to us?
13. Why is it a duty for the soul-winner to strive to draw
    men to himself personally,—to be liked, in other words?

[1] Page 86.

SEEKING COMMON INTERESTS

(For study before reading this chapter)

1. If a worldly man whom you wanted to win should ask you what you meant by "being saved," what answer would you give?

2. What has Christ's salvation to do with this life and the affairs of this life?

3. Did Christ himself emphasize chiefly men's future or present need of him? Illustrate by Gospel passages.

4. Give your own definition of saving faith.

5. Should you say it is usually hard or easy to become interested in another's interests?

6. When you are seeking to win one whose creed or denominational tendencies may be quite different from your own, what is your best course?

7. Are any interests of another too trifling for us to utilize? How draw the line between worthy and unworthy interests of another? How far should we be willing to go in entering into another's activities in order to win him?

V

SEEKING COMMON INTERESTS

A CHRISTIAN man was urging his friend to give himself to the Saviour. "I know you do not believe you can save yourself," said the first; "do you know of any other Saviour than Jesus Christ?"

The man thus questioned faced his friend squarely, and said, "May I ask you a question? What do you mean by being saved?"

Then it was that the first speaker had to consider, more carefully, perhaps, than he had ever done before, though he had from boyhood been a confessed follower of Christ, what he *did* mean by being "saved." To show any vagueness or uncertainty in defining his belief would be disastrous at that moment, to his influence with the one whom he longed to help. Yet he believed that it would be equally disastrous to use "stock phrases" with this man, who from his boyhood had been brought up in a Christian home of exceptional strictness, and who was, as he claimed, too familiar with conventional religious views and talk to be otherwise than antagonized by them. Other circumstances added to the difficulty. The man was, far beyond the average, clean-lived, morally high-toned, honorable, aspiring, interested in the best things. But he was not at all sure that there is any life beyond the present, nor did he find the average church or preaching of special interest to him.

The critically important thing for the soul-winner to do, at this point, was to answer the honest question in terms of the present interests of the questioner. His first move was to put a counter-question.

"Are you satisfied with yourself?" he asked.

" Not by a good deal," came the unhesitating reply.

" I knew you well enough to be sure of that," said the first man. " Have you always been able to accomplish what you want to accomplish in your life?"

" Far from it," was the answer.

" Let me tell you, then, what I mean by being saved," said the one who was urging the Good Tidings. " I have never found a man yet who was satisfied with himself. And I have never found any one who satisfied me, except Jesus Christ. I discovered long ago that I could not live a single day satisfactorily in my own strength. Christ has enabled me to come nearer to my best than I have ever been able to do alone. By being ' saved,' I mean saved to one's best, enabled to make one's life count for the most. That is what the Saviour has done for me."

A very inadequate and " temporal " definition of salvation, you say? Certainly, it was only a partial definition, but it was enough to set thinking in a new line a man who had hitherto supposed the Christian's idea of salvation to be chiefly the holding of a golden harp, and freedom from hell fire, through eternity. Indeed, he answered at once with heartiness, " I am glad to hear you say that. I am glad you did not say anything about the next world, for, frankly, I haven't any use for the regulation views of endless punishment and that sort of thing."

A little later the friend who had presented the sub-

ject of salvation as being something of present value
in this present world took occasion to make clear to
the other that he had no uncertain convictions as to
the next world, and as to this life being only a beginning or preparation for the next. There was no argument or discussion on this point, nor on any other.
But it would clearly have been unwise to urge the question of salvation in relation to the life beyond as the
first thing for consideration by one who had, or
claimed to have, doubts as to a life beyond. The man
was willing to admit his need of help in this life. From
that as a starting-point it was well to begin.

Making Salvation of Present Interest

And there is a truth emphasized by this incident
that ought to have large place in the thoughts of every
confessed follower of Christ. Are we not too much
inclined to relegate salvation to the next world, as a
kind of benefit payable upon death, the definite securing of which was finally accomplished when we stood
up and confessed the Saviour before men, and the
principal value of which is for another world than this?
Our Lord said nothing about men needing him more
after death than in present life. He did say, of
Zacchæus, " *To-day* is salvation come to this house."
And he added, " For the Son of man came to seek
and to save that which *was* lost,"—not " which was
to be lost."

To be " saved," then, means that present life here
on the earth becomes a different thing. It means
that the disappointing struggle to which the unsaved
are doomed in this life, and to which the exceptionally moral man already referred to confessed as his

own experience, shall give way to a life of achieving
something that brings satisfaction instead of dissatis-
faction. It does not mean that we are going to be
satisfied with ourselves, nor satisfied with our work.
But it means that we have found a Person, a Saviour,
with whom we can be satisfied, and in whose service
assured victory, as over against continued defeat, is
found. It means that life takes on a fulness, a richness, an abundance, that is possible only through that
Saviour. If one who has not accepted this salvation
asks, " How am I to know this? Why should I believe it?" the answer comes from Christ's followers
with ringing, triumphant confidence, " We know it
because we have tried it. You may know it for yourself if you will." It is not necessary to make the service of Christ seem an easy thing, for it is not. But it is
important to make the way of salvation simple. Remember Bushnell's definition of faith: " Faith is that
act by which one person, a sinner, commits himself
to another Person, a Saviour." Any one can understand that.

Not only at the moment of approach is it important
to be thinking of the other man's interests in order to
begin with them, but the principle holds throughout
the work of soul-winning. We must not only begin
there; we may have to stay there for a long time if we
would exert any influence that is really to count for
Christ. This truth is unmistakably emphasized in the
New Testament. Not only at the beginning of the
apostles' ministry were others drawn to them " because
that every man heard them speaking in his own language....speaking in our tongues the mighty works

of God," [1] but Paul evidently made this a permanent principle of his evangelistic work:

> For though I was free from all men, I brought myself under bondage to all, that I might gain the more. And to the Jews I became as a Jew, that I might gain Jews; to them that are under the law, as under the law, not being myself under the law, that I might gain them that are under the law; to them that are without law, as without law, not being without law to God, but under law to Christ, that I might gain them that are without law. To the weak I became weak, that I might gain the weak: I am become all things to all men, that I may by all means save some. [2]

Were not these the tactics he had in mind as he wrote later to the same converts:

> And I will most gladly spend and be spent for your souls. If I love you more abundantly, am I loved the less? But be it so, I did not myself burden you; but, being crafty, I caught you with guile. [3]

There is the guile, the bait, the deep-laid planning that Christ and Paul used and that we must learn how to use, most gladly spending and being spent if we would hope to take men alive. The work was costly to them; there will be little virtue in our work unless we make it costly to ourselves. The question is not, "Am I naturally interested in this person and his interests?" but "Am I willing to *get* interested?" For we always can if we will.

And it is always possible to disarm antagonism and win confidence by this sinking of self-interests and deliberate cultivating of another's interests. An instance of this occurred in a boarding-house experience:

[1] Acts 2: 6, 11.

[2] 1 Corinthians 9: 19-22. [3] 2 Corinthians 12: 15, 16.

One winter, some time after the Civil War, I passed a number of weeks in a Southern city, with a young friend who was necessitated to be there for his health. All this time we were at a well-filled boarding-house. Most of the persons there were those whom I then met for the first time. A young gentleman who sat just opposite me at the table, and with whom I naturally came to have a speaking acquaintance, was a person whose habits of life and ordinary occupations were obviously different from mine, so that our sympathy would not be promoted by conferring over these. Indeed, I learned, from the proprietor of the house, that when he understood that a New England army chaplain was coming to the house as a boarder he wanted to leave the house on that account, and was only prevented from doing so by the crowded state of that winter resort.

This certainly did not present an attractive opening for personal religious conversation. Yet I had learned that God gives us opportunities and responsibilities, in this line, which are of his choosing rather than of ours; so I waited for signs of God's leading. Meantime I endeavored to show to my table-mate that we had things in common that were to be recognized and enjoyed. To win his confidence to me was a duty, if I would hope to lead him toward Christ.[1]

When, after some weeks of this intercourse, the time came for the chaplain to leave, he realized that he must now or perhaps never speak the direct personal word for which he had been trying to prepare the way. He reproached himself for not having done so earlier, yet even now he was in doubt as to whether he had won the man sufficiently to make his words of any avail.

I spoke of the matter to my room-mate and companion, for whose health I was at the South. I suggested that perhaps it was my duty to go to the room of my fellow-boarder that very afternoon, and say a word to him for Christ. He might,

[1] Pages 56-58.

indeed, take offense at it, but, again, he might not. Was it not worth while taking such a risk for a soul's sake, and for Christ's? The decision was made. We kneeled together in our room, and asked God's blessing on my undertaking. Then I arose and started out. The room of my fellow-boarder and his wife was but just across the hall from ours. Yet it was not an easy task to venture on knocking at that room door, in the fulfilment of my purpose and my duty.

At my knock, the young gentleman whom I sought opened the door, and invited me in. His wife sat on a sofa. They welcomed me cordially, and when I told them that I purposed leaving the place the next morning early, they expressed regret, saying that our intercourse of the past few weeks had been very pleasant. I replied that I had enjoyed knowing them, and that it was because of my growing personal interest in them that I had now called at their room. Then I explained that my joy in Christ's service was the greatest possession of my life, and that because I longed for my fellow-boarders to have that joy, I had come to say so. The gentleman said that it was kind of me to say this, and that he had been thinking that he would like to know more about the religious belief I had, so that he might share it. Would I tell him what books he should read, in order to learn about this?

I replied that I could mention good books for him, but that I should much prefer to talk on the subject with him personally in detail.

"It would be very pleasant," he said, "to put myself under your guidance, if you would instruct me."

"But I leave town early to-morrow morning," I said, "and I am cut off by this from helping you."

On his asking where I was going, and learning that I was to visit another part of the South, he responded that he would be glad to accompany me. On his asking his wife if that would be agreeable to her, she expressed her willingness to make the move, and it was arranged accordingly. Early the next morning the boarder who had wanted to leave that house when he found that a clergyman was coming there, with whom he could have no sympathy, finally left the house with that clergyman in order that he might be personally instructed in the religion which he had come to desire as his own possession. Surely God was leading. And God ever leads those who are willing to be led, even though they often follow reluctantly! [1]

But—and one may say it in all reverence—God himself could not have led to this result unless a child of his had been ready to pay the cost of studying and seeking another's temporal interests, in order that, by guile, he might be led to higher and better things.

Ignoring Differences of Creed

There can be no barrier between any two men sufficient to prevent their finding common ground if only one of the two is determined that they shall. Least of all need differences of creed or faith keep men apart, though these are often allowed to do so.

When God brings us alongside of one whom we may help, or may feel a responsibility for, we are not to consider the obstacles, or difficulties, in the way. God will take care of them. Nor are we to be hindered by religious or denominational differences that seem to stand between us and him. The question is not whether he is a Roman Catholic, or a Jew, a Muhammadan, a Mormon, a Maronite, or an infidel. But the one question is, Can we evidence to him, in such a way as to impress on him, and to deepen his sense of their preciousness, the surpassing love of God and the blessed fulness of the spirit of Christ? We are not to risk the repelling of him by making prominent the things wherein we differ; but we are to approach him at the one "point of contact," that from a connection at that point the electric current of sympathy may quiver to the extremities of his very being.

In my limited experience with humanity I have had occasion to meet and converse as to personal religion with individuals of every one of the above-named religions, or non-religion, as well as with many others; and I have never found our differences a real barrier to our converse or to the cordial recognition of our real heart sympathy. "Every heart is human," and God's love is suited to the need of every human heart. Our duty is to follow God's lead, nothing doubting.

One winter Sunday morning, in a country place in Eastern Massachusetts, I found myself a guest in the home of the superintendent of a Sunday-school, at the anniversary of which I was to speak in the afternoon. In the forenoon of that day I was to address a congregation several miles from my present stopping-place. My host was to send me over, in his home team, for my forenoon appointment. Accordingly I found myself, that very cold day, tucked in, under a heavy robe, in close quarters, in the buggy, with the Irish driver. It was evident that that man was just then the "every creature" in the world for me to teach the gospel to, and I had no right to expect a blessing on my labors for the rest of the day if I failed in my duty to him while on my way to my next appointment.

To begin with, I told my seat-mate whither and why I was going. This was to indicate my confidence in him. Then I said, as showing my interest in him and his standpoint:

"You are a Catholic, I suppose?"

"Yes, sir," was his reply, with a tone that seemed to indicate a conscious barrier between us.

I at once spoke of several Roman Catholic bishops and priests with whom I was intimate, and whom I valued, and then asked:

"Have you a Catholic Church in the village?"—which we had just left.

"There is no church there yet, sir. But a priest comes over once in four weeks, and says mass."

"When is the next time for his coming?" I asked.

"He's there to-day, sir."

"Then I'm keeping you away from mass. How sorry I am for this!"

"Oh! it's all right, sir. I'm glad to go with you, sir."

We were on the same plane by this time. It was now my duty to improve this advantage. And I began:

"You say you're a Catholic; are you a good Catholic?

Do you honestly love God, and trust your blessed Saviour, as you are taught, by your church, is your duty?"

"I'm afraid I'm not a good Catholic, sir. I'm afraid I do not do my duty."

What better start could you ask for an earnest talk with a nominal Protestant, if he were known to be cold and indifferent, or a backslider, and you wanted to arouse him to deep and intense feeling in the truth of truths? At this starting-point I pressed home the truth:

"My friend, when we think of what the blessed Jesus did for us, how he left his glorious home in heaven, and became a babe in a manger to begin with, and then toiled on here and suffered for years, and was despised and rejected of men, and was crucified and died, in proof of his love for us, and of his Father's love, in order that we can be saved, is it asking or expecting too much of us that we should show our gratitude in the little things that Christ asks of us?"

"No, sir, it is not."

And of this sacred theme we talked together pleasantly, on that carriage seat, that Sunday morning, until we reached our destination. My new host, a clergyman, welcomed me to his home, while he directed the driver, with his horse, to the stable. On entering the parsonage, I said to the pastor that, as the day was very cold, I should be glad to have the driver invited into the kitchen out of the cold. Accordingly, he went to the barn to invite the man in. Returning, the pastor told me that the man said he wished to go to church to hear the gentleman preach that he had just brought over.

As I rose in the pulpit, I saw my seat-mate of the morning facing me in a pew. What he had heard from me about his Saviour, and about his duty to that Saviour, had apparently sharpened his appetite for more. I confess that some of the words of my address that morning were for that one hearer, rather than for the body of the congregation. Then, as at many times before and since, one person was more to me than many persons. As, at noon, we drove back together, our conversation was again on the theme of themes, with fresh comments on phases of it about which I had talked, in his hearing, from the pulpit.

On thinking the day's work over at its close, I realized,

not that a Protestant and a Roman Catholic had found much that they could talk about together to their mutual spiritual profit, but that we two, who had met together as seat-mates on that cold Sunday morning's ride, might have been profited by the talk even had we been two Presbyterian elders in conference in revival time.[1]

Going Where the Other Man Is

The secret of getting successfully interested in another is simply that we deliberately put ourselves mentally into that one's place. It takes mental effort, and sacrifice of easy-going comfort to do this, but not exceptional genius. The old story of the lost horse is a familiar one. The whole village had turned out to find the horse, but had failed. Finally a youth who had the reputation of being somewhat feeble-minded led the horse home. Upon being plied with questions as to how he had done what every one else had failed to do, he quietly explained. He had first ascertained where the horse had last been seen. "Then I went there," he said, "and I just said to myself, 'now where would I go if I was a horse?' And I went there, and there he was." It was not only a simple method, but the only one. We have got to learn to go where the other fellow is if we want to find him.

An incident in a well-known pastor's experience illustrates this with telling effectiveness:

"Yes, I want to come into the church; have been wanting to come for fifteen years," a woman said to the minister when he urged her to confess Christ at the next communion. "But I'm waiting for Jim. You know he's a good man, yet he doesn't have much use for the church, or—begging your pardon —for preachers. He tells me to go ahead, and stop waiting for

[1] Pages 46 50.

him. Many a time I've made up my mind to do just that.
Then, at the last minute, I think if I wait just a little while
longer, surely he'll come with me. What would you do?"

The visitor told her the best thing she could do would be
to become a church member without further delay, for she
would have a better chance to influence her husband as a professed Christian than as an outsider. Before the call was con-
cluded, she agreed that this was her best course.

As the minister left, he said, " Please remember me to Mr.
B. when he comes home, tell him I am sorry to have missed
him, and that I hope to have a good talk with him soon."

A few days later he met Mrs. B. once more. " Jim made
me promise to tell you something for him," she said, much
embarrassed. " He says if you want to see him so much you
will just have to go where he is."

" And where is that?" was the inquiry.

" Hadn't you better wait a few days before going to
him? Then he'll be where the likes of you can get to him
better. You see, to-day he's working on the last section of the
steeple of the new church."

It was enough. The minister made up his mind he would
find Jim that very afternoon. At the church—a magnificent
building with a lofty spire—he learned that his quarry was
indeed at the top. " You can't get to him—though; nothing
but ladders to climb on; better let us call him down," the
foreman suggested.

But the minister had been challenged to go where Jim
was. So he climbed ladder after ladder until—nearly two
hundred feet above the street—he found a much-surprised man.
A few minutes were spent in very satisfactory conversa:.un.
Then the minister climbed down to make other calls.

The next Sunday Jim became a member of the church his
wife had already joined, and was thereafter known as an
earnest Christian man. His friends wondered a little at the
change in his life; but the only explanation he would give
was this :—

" The preacher who'll climb two hundred feet of ladders
to call on me can have me every time!" [1]

[1] The Rev. John T. Faris, in The Sunday School Times.

A young man of pronounced agnosticism but of scholarly scientific interests one time came into Dr. Trumbull's horizon. There was no common ground at all, in spiritual matters, to begin with. The older man, however, learned—by making it his business to learn—that the younger student was deeply interested in a certain line of scientific study. Promptly he set out to know something of that subject himself. He spent some weeks in reading it up. He gathered books on it, every one he could lay his hands on, and put them by. Then one day he mentioned to the young student that he had several books in that field at his office, and he invited him to avail himself of them whenever he cared to look them over. The subject became a theme of mutual interest, and the younger man eagerly seized opportunities of discussing it with one who knew so much more about it than most persons he met. From that common ground, reached only by the costly sacrifice of time and study by the soul-winner, it was not difficult to lead on to spiritual matters; and the day came when the once-agnostic thanked God and his confessed Saviour that one man had been willing to be " all things " to him.

This seeking of the " other fellow's " interests was a secret of the success of the founder of the Young Men's Christian Association, Sir George Williams. His biographer tells a characteristic incident of his young manhood:

George Williams was possessed also of that extraordinarily rare virtue in a young man—tact. He was wont to say, when asked as to the means he suggested for tackling a young man, " Don't argue, take him to supper," and in more than one instance he carried out his suggestion literally. In reviewing these early days, George Williams used to tell the story of how they won over to their side one of the young fellows in the house who was most active in his opposition, and whose conduct was a terrible ordeal for their faith. He held a good position in the business, and, as George Williams relates, "we could not get near him in any way. When any young fellow gave his heart to Christ, he would pounce upon him and say, 'We'll soon take all that nonsense out of you!'"

This young man was the organizer and chairman of the "free-and-easy" held on Saturday evening at the adjoining public-house, "The Goose and Gridiron," and largely frequented by Hitchcock & Rogers's assistants. In a short time he had promoted a very active and vigorous campaign against these young men of the upper room, and naturally he was at once marked out by them for special and particular prayer. For many weeks they waited in vain for sign of change. His hostility increased in vehemence and bitterness.

The best part of one evening's meeting was devoted to a discussion as the most likely means of getting into touch with this most unsympathetic young man.

"Can any one tell me," said George Williams, "if there is anything he is especially fond of which we could give him? Can we do anything that will overcome his dislike for us?" One of those present suggested with a touch of humor that he had a passion for oysters.

"Let's give him an oyster supper, then," said George Williams. "Who is the best man to invite him?"

They selected one who was on comparatively friendly terms with the chairman of the "free-and-easy," and in due course he was casually informed that a number of the young fellows were going to join in a big oyster supper, and would be glad if he would accompany them. The idea of these Christian young men indulging in such frivolity amused him immensely, and in a spirit of bravado he accepted their invitation.

It was a lively evening for all concerned, and all enjoyed it, for George Williams had given strict instructions that no attempt at proselytising was to be made on that occasion. Their avowed enemy, finding himself in such pleasant company, came to the conclusion that these young men were not so black as he had painted them. As a return for their hospitality, he consented later on to attend one of their meetings. The sequel is best told in an extract from the diary of George Williams's friend, Edgar Valentine, who writes in May, 1844:

"In the course of the day George Williams came to me and said he believed something particular was going to happen to-day, inasmuch as the Spirit's operation seemed visible in our midst. A young man by the name of Rogers was seriously impressed about his soul's salvation. G. W. spoke to him after we had arranged to have a prayer-meeting in the evening, and whilst engaged packing up a parcel Rogers came to me and told me that he was thinking very seriously about his immortal soul."

The next morning Rogers was still more concerned, and William Creese, noticing his attitude, said to George Williams, "George, what is up with Rogers?" "I do not know," he replied, "but I feel I cannot pray for him any longer. I was praying for him this morning until it seemed as if I heard a voice from heaven saying to me 'Yes,' and I knew he would be converted." Shortly afterwards Rogers definitely threw in his lot with the little band of the upper room. His name is to be found among the first twelve members of the Association.[1]

The question sometimes arises as to whether a soul-winner may properly interest himself in any and every interest of another man's in order to influence and win him. The answer to that question is plain and unmistakable. One may devote himself to any interest under the sun that is not actually wrong or harmful in its effects. It is never necessary to depart one jot or one tittle from Christ's standards in order to win men's confidence. But it is often necessary to depart a long way from our own natural interests in order to meet another on common ground. We must never let down; we must often go far afield. Here

[1] From "The Life of Sir George Williams," by J. E. Hodder Williams, pages 98-101.

is the difference between playing a game of tennis with a man in order to reach him, and playing a game of cards; or between letting a man smoke or drink in your presence without a word of criticism, though courteously declining his invitation to join him, as over against the fatal mistake of supposing that you would gain in influence with him by indulging in what you know and he knows (or will know later) is against your principles.

Another question that is sometimes asked, especially in the case of a busy minister, is whether one may not make the mistake of spending too much time over the temporal interests of a single individual in the hope of leading him eventually to Christ. Should a pastor, for example, spend a solid half-day, or day, or even more, in getting work for a man out of a job, in order to prove to that man his genuine interest in his bodily welfare, and with the purpose of winning the man to Christ, when that pastor might in the same time speak a word for Christ to perhaps a score of other souls? In other words, shall we choose the touch-and-go method, or the slower, costlier plan?

Can there be any real doubt as to which method has Christ's approval? The touch-and-go plan will have just about as much effectiveness as the lightness of its words imply. We are not in this work chiefly for arithmetical results. Christ did not work that way. Once let men get the impression that a pastor or a neighbor cares only for their souls and not at all for their bodies, and his influence over them is gone. As Wilfred T. Grenfell, the sturdy young English physician who is giving his life to reclaiming the bodies and souls of the Labrador fisherfolk, has said: " Is not the real problem of Christianity how best to commend it to the world? Can we afford to divorce the ' secular ' from the ' religious,' any more than the ' religious ' from the ' secular '? It seems to me there is only one way to reach the soul—that is, through the body. For when the soul has cast off the body we cannot reach it at all."

Topics and Questions for Study and Discussion

(To test one's grasp of the contents of the chapter)

1. Give a definition of salvation that should appeal to a man who claims to be in doubt about the next world.
2. What mistake of emphasis should we avoid in talking and thinking of spiritual matters?
3. Give Bushnell's definition of faith.
4. How long may we need to study another man's interests in winning him to Christ?
5. Quote Paul's statement as to the importance of seeking others' interests in seeking to save them.
6. What is necessary to the removing of a barrier which is preventing two men from finding common ground?
7. When talking with one whose creed differs from our own, is it well to emphasize the differences of belief, or to emphasize points of agreement? Why?
8. What common ground can always be found between Protestants and Catholics?
9. What common ground should you say can always be found between Jews and Christians?
10. What is there in our going where the other man is that is likely to attract him to us?
11. What suggestive advice of six words was Sir George Williams fond of giving to soul-winners?
12. How far may we go in identifying ourselves with another's interests?
13. What did Grenfell say as to our duty of giving prominent attention to men's bodies and secular interests?

THE PLACE OF THE BIBLE
IN THIS WORK

(For study before reading this chapter)

1. What is your own thought as to the use of Scripture quotations in individual soul-winning?
2. Is there any danger of a tendency to use the Bible as a fetish? Give illustrations of such use. How should that danger be guarded against?
3. Wherein is the Bible like other books?
4. Wherein is the Bible different from all other books?
5. Under what circumstances should you say a Bible quotation would be most effective?
6. Under what circumstances should you say a Bible quotation would be least effective?
7. Now formulate a principle for the use of the Bible in individual soul-winning.

VI

THE PLACE OF THE BIBLE IN
THIS WORK

T HE Bible is the soul-winner's indispensable equipment. But it is not necessarily his tool. A moment's consideration of the principles already studied
will show why. Ninety-nine persons in a hundred, of
those who have not yet come to Christ, are not deeply
interested in the Bible. A Bible text is not, as yet,
attractive bait to them. The fact that the Bible *ought*
to be attractive to them has nothing to do with the
matter. We are working with men as they are, not
with men as they ought to be. If they were already
just where they ought to be in their interests, they
would be in no need of our attention.

Recognizing, therefore, that the Bible and its teachings have little place in the chief interests of the great
number of those whom we would reach: if we would
use bait that shall attract them at the outset, and seek
interests that are common to them and ourselves, we
must, as a rule, begin with something else than a Bible
quotation.

This principle was one of Christ's principles in the
work of individual soul-winning,[1] and is in accordance
with all that we know of human nature, and of God's

---

[1] See page 179, Chapter IX. of this volume.

approved ways of dealing with men. It underlies successful man-winning in every sphere of life. Don't expect the man whom you would win to begin with your interests; begin with his.

Apply the test to some of the actual instances of successful soul-winning that we have already studied. Take the case of the whiskey-drinking seat-mate in the railroad train.[1] What would have been the outcome if, after the flask had been proffered, the soul-winner had begun his conversation with the impressive words, " wine is a mocker, strong drink is raging." Probably some such answer as, " Then I guess I'll do my raging back in the smoker, stranger," and that day's opportunity would have come to an abrupt ending with the man's exit.

Or suppose the young army chaplain, hitherto unknown to the profane old skipper in charge of the perilous transport expedition,[2] had introduced himself that evening with any of these phrases: " Swear not at all." " Let your speech be Yea, yea; Nay, nay." " Thou shalt not take the name of the Lord thy God in vain." Just what likelihood is there that the skipper would have been so won to the stranger as to have offered him his cabin for that night?

The point is not that those Scripture passages do not contain truth which those two men sorely needed to consider. But the men were in no state of mind to listen to Scripture passages at the outset. Later on, when that old skipper had " come as a little child to be a disciple of Jesus," he probably treasured some of those very Scripture passages as safeguards of his life. But this was because he had been talked to first of all in his " own language," which was not the language of the Bible, and about his own interests, which were not yet Scriptural or spiritual.

H. Clay Trumbull's Habit

Dr. Trumbull was a devoted Bible-student from the time of his conversion till the day of his death. So absorbing a place did Bible-study fill in his life that he believed he might be permitted to continue his Bible studies in the next world. His regular daily plan of Bible reading was to read the Book through from Genesis to Revelation, short sections at a time, turning back to Genesis to begin again after he had finished. In this way he read and studied and re-read and re-studied every word of the Scriptures through a long lifetime. He drew his strength and knowledge, his convictions, his hopes, his guidance and his life, from the pages of that book. The writer has the little pocket Bible, in its tattered buckskin case, which the army chaplain kept close to him as more of a protection than his sword and his pistol during the dark days of the Civil War.

Yet an examination of the experiences in individual soul-winning that are the basis of our present study shows that Dr. Trumbull rarely *quoted* Scripture when he was first seeking to win another to Christ. The reasons for this we have already seen.

Although the writer had talked over with his father many of the incidents described in " Individual Work," he had never happened to ask him specifically his thought as to the place of Bible-quoting in this work. The conviction as to the principle suggested in this chapter was simply the result of inductive study of the facts. It was the more interesting and significant, therefore, when, three years after Dr. Trumbull's death, there was discovered the following letter that the author of " Individual Work " had written on this very question to a stranger at a distance who had asked his advice. The letter was written in the last year of Dr. Trumbull's life. It is interesting, also, to note the emphasis upon the principle that " one is more than many."

February 2, 1903.

MY DEAR BROTHER:

Your kind letter interests me, and I thank you for your pleasant words. I am indeed glad that anything I have written has been of service to you or to those whom you know.

As to the questions you ask, I fear I may startle you, if not indeed shock you by frank answers. I was never a theological student nor a pastor. My training has been wholly practical, among men as they are. I have been an army chaplain and a Sunday-school worker. Hence, my ways are unconventional; and not like those you are taught in the books.

(1) I have not been in the habit of using Bible texts or Bible language in my talks with individuals. I talk in the most natural and direct way with my fellows about their duty and their desires. If I used a Bible text, some conventional or erroneous meaning may have attached to it by the person to whom I am speaking. I seek help, and, in a sense inspiration, from the God of the Bible; but I want everything fresh from him for the case in hand.

(2) In seeking to develop a local church along this line, I should give myself to one man of that church. One man is more to me than a thousand in this matter. When he is won it is time to think of another. If I thought of two men at the same time, I might fail to give myself wholly to the one I was living to win.

(3) I think that most local churches consider souls as more important than a soul. In consequence, an aroused

Christian is more desirous of seeing a great revival than of winning to Christ the one soul who ought to be revived. Yet a good deal depends on whether the mission of a local church is to train souls in Christ's service, or to win outside souls to Christ. In either case, work must be directed accordingly.

As you asked me about these three points I tell you frankly my thought on the subject, without saying that you ought to, or are likely to, think the same way.

Cordially and fraternally yours,

H. CLAY TRUMBULL.

When the Bible is Common Meeting-Ground

Of course, if we find, as we may in an exceptional case, one who is not Christ's confessed follower yet who is greatly interested in the Bible, then the Bible may be the very meeting-ground of common interest that we can properly seek. Such an unusual case as this is notably illustrated in the following experience of the Rev. George F. Pentecost, D.D.:

It was in the Chicago Tabernacle. The inquiry-rooms had been crowded all the evening. It was now about eleven o'clock, and most of the workers and inquirers had gone home. A few, however, of both classes were lingering still. I had just left a man—a straightforward German—who had given himself up to God through Jesus Christ; and was about leaving the room, not seeing that there was anything more for me to do, when I was approached by a young Christian, who said:

"Mr. Pentecost, before you go, won't you come and speak to that young man?" (pointing to him). "I do not seem to be able to meet his need."

"Certainly," said I, and went over to where the young man was seated; and drawing a chair up to him, said:

"Can I be of any help to you, my brother?"

"I don't know, I am sure; but if you can give me any help, I will gratefully receive it."

A few questions developed the fact that he was a cul-

tivated young German, the son of a German rationalistic theo-
logian. He had been but a short time in America. He was
thoroughly conversant with the current Continental sceptical
philosophies. He told me that he was fond of study, and especially philosophical study; and gave good evidence of familiarity with the various schools of thought, current and
past. He said he had been led to think of Christianity as an
ingenious mythology (having a very slender thread of historical truth in it), more or less the product of an early enthusiasm that had exalted Jesus into Deity. He confessed that
he had never made the New Testament a study, but had im-
bibed his opinions mainly from Strauss. He went on to say
that he had been attracted by curiosity into the Tabernacle;
and had been amazed at the vast audiences held together week
after week, without excitement, simply by the proclamation
of Christian truths, and the recital of Bible stories. He admitted that he was impressed with the matter of Mr. Moody's
preaching, and was convinced from his manner that he was a
sincere and honest teacher.

Finally, he determined to take up the New Testament,
and carefully read it. He had done so; and this night he had
come into the inquiry-room to seek conversation with some
Christian who would explain, if it were possible, some of the
chief difficulties that he met with in the New Testament. He
was altogether frank and candid, saying that he was free to
admit that a careful reading of the New Testament revealed
a purer and altogether better system of ethics than that of
any of the philosophies with which he was acquainted; and
that the whole book had an air of sincerity and truth about it.
But there were several insuperable difficulties in the way
of his acceptance of it as truth.

I asked him to state his difficulties, which he did in about
these words:

"There are three chief claims set forth in the New Testament, upon the truth of which, it seems to me, the whole
system must stand or fall."

"What are they?"

"Why, first of all, it is claimed all through the New Testament that Jesus was the Son of God; *i. e.,* God manifested
in human nature—a supernatural Being. This he claimed for

himself, and even died in defense of the claim; for, if I am not mistaken, that was the charge upon which he was put to death by the Jews; viz., that in claiming to be the Son of God he made himself to be equal with God—which was, under the Jewish law, blasphemy. Certainly he seems to have believed himself to be God; and so also did his apostles, especially John and Paul."

"Well, what is your next difficulty?"

"Why, the next difficulty is that our salvation depends, not upon the uprightness of our own lives, but upon the fact of Christ's death, which is represented as a sacrificial act—what Mr. Moody calls 'the atonement.'"

"Well, what is the other difficulty?"

"The resurrection of Christ from the dead. Everything in Christianity depends upon that."

"Well," said I, "now why are these things difficulties to you?"

"Why, I cannot possibly believe that Jesus was God. He could not be. And it is not possible for any one who was *really* dead to rise again. Such a thing never was in the world, and it could not be. And even if it were so, I do not see how any one could be saved on account of another's death, and not on account of his own uprightness."

I confess that the task before me seemed very great indeed. But he seemed guileless in his desire to know the truth; and so, with a prayer in my heart for help, I said:

"Well now, let us look at the first difficulty—the incarnation. As I understand it, you are a Theist. You believe in the existence of a personal, eternal, and omnipotent God, who is the Author of the universe and of our being?"

"Oh, yes!"

"Very well. Now, with that for a starting point, you cannot philosophically hold that the incarnation is an *impossibility—that it could not be.*"

A very little talk ended in his admitting the *possibility* of the incarnation, but denying the *probability* of it. And then he went on to say, with the quickness of thought and the clearest perception of the whole matter:

"But I think Jesus was himself deceived. I grant that he may have, in moments of enthusiasm, thought he was the

Son of God; and that he did at times make this claim there
is no doubt. But at other times he certainly made such statements as forbid us, on his own testimony, to believe that he
was equal with God; indeed, he admits that he is an inferior
being. In fact, Christ's own testimony concerning himself is
contradictory.

"And this leads me to question the truth of the Gospels;
and so to reject Christ as the Son of God, and hence Christianity itself. For Christianity is nothing but a beautiful de-
lusion, if Christ is not what he claims to be. Now he says in
one place, 'I and my Father are one' (John 10:30); and
again, 'He that hath seen me hath seen the Father' (John
14:9); and, as I have before said, when on trial before the
high priest he still claimed, and that in the face of certain
death, that he was the Son of God. (Mark 14:62; Matt.
26:64.) But he said on another occasion that his Father
was greater than he. (John 14:28.) Now he cannot be one
with God, and at the same time inferior to God. And he
says, 'All power is given unto me.' (Matt. 28:18.) Now that
is an admission that he had not power *himself*, but it was
given to him; and surely he that *receives* power is inferior to
him that *gives* it. Now are not these contradictions in his
own testimony? And do not they destroy the worth of it
entirely? It seems to me that, whatever of truth there may be
in the historical existence of Jesus Christ, he only *imagined*
that he was the Son of God; and that in speaking of himself,
he spoke according to the *mood* he was in, sometimes believing himself to be the Son of God."

After hearing him through, I turned to the passages he
had referred to, and having read them aloud, I said:

"Let us suppose that you had been on earth when Jesus
was here, and had heard him make these contradictory (?)
statements; and had asked him, saying, 'Master, I do not
quite understand you. A little while ago you said, "I and my
Father are one," and, "He that hath seen me hath seen the
Father;" and again you say, "My Father is greater than I,"
and, "All power is *given* me." How can you be one with
the Father, and yet less than the Father? And how can you be
equal with the Father, if your power is given to you, and not
yours independently?' And suppose he had said in reply,

'My child, what if, *for the purpose of your redemption* from sin and the curse of the law, I *voluntarily laid aside my eternal glory,* and suffered myself to be born of a woman, and made under the law, thus *limiting my being* to the *conditions of your nature,* that I might, in that nature, offer up to God such a sacrifice for sin as would enable him to proclaim forgiveness of sins to the whole world? In such a case can you not conceive that there is no contradiction in these sayings of mine? For, indeed, *I am* one with the Father, and he that hath seen me hath seen the Father; but for purposes of atonement I have *voluntarily assumed an inferior position,* that I might thus take your place and die, which I could not have done unless I had taken a subordinate place, yea, and your very nature. Thus I sometimes speak of my *eternal relation to God,* and sometimes of my relation to him as the *messenger of the covenant* sent forth to redeem.'"

He listened attentively to this; and then said, as if speaking to himself:

"Yes, that might be; I can see how that might be. But" (speaking to me) "did Christ ever make such an explanation? Is that the theory of Christ's subordination to the Father?"

In answer to this inquiry I turned to the second chapter of Philippians, and said:

"Certainly this is the explanation of it; for see, Paul was trying to inculcate lessons of humility, by exhorting the Philippians to voluntarily take a subordinate place in relation to each other, though they might, as a matter of fact and right, stand on an equality; and enforced his exhortation by this reference, 'Let this mind be in you, which was also in Christ Jesus; who, being in the form of God, thought it not robbery to be equal with God' (thought not his equality with God something to be contended for) : 'but *made himself* of no reputation, and took upon him the form of a servant, and was made in the likeness of men: and being found in fashion as a man, *he humbled himself,* and became obedient unto death, even the death of the cross.'" (Phil. 2: 5-8.)

He took my Bible in his hand, and read the passage over and over himself, and said: "Wonderful! wonderful!" And still holding the book in his hand, with quivering chin and moistened eyes, he said:

" Yes, the Son of God made himself of no reputation FOR
ME; *and took my nature, and died on the cross* FOR ME *!"*

And then, looking up into my face, he said:

" What have I got to do about it? "

To which I replied:

" Accept him; believe on him; and confess him as your
Saviour."

" May I? "

I replied, opening my Bible to Romans 10:9: " If thou
shalt confess with thy mouth the Lord Jesus, and shalt
believe in thine heart that God hath raised him from the
dead, thou shalt be saved."

" Let me see that! "

I handed him the book, and he read it aloud, and then
said:

" I do believe in my heart that God raised him from the
dead; and I do acknowledge him as my Saviour."

We dropped down together upon our knees (with a little
group which had gathered about us); and I offered a brief
prayer of thanksgiving to God for his conversion, and a little
petition for his keeping.

Thus was the young Rationalist converted.

It will be seen at a glance that no attempt was made to
meet his objections by an exhaustive argument, but by simply
presenting the biblical statement to him, leaving the work
of conviction to the Holy Spirit. As a mere argument, the
statement may have been very defective; but God can take
his own truth and use it more mightily than the strongest
argument man can construct.

The exceptional features of this case are to be
noted. The man who was won had come of his own
accord, because of his interest in Christianity, to a
place where he hoped to get light. He was interested
in the Bible at second-hand, and needed only wise
guidance to the truths of the Bible at first hand. He
had specific difficulties of interpretation of Christianity; when those difficulties were met by one whose
familiarity with the whole Bible enabled him to meet

them, the man's course was clear. Without such Bible-knowledge, Dr. Pentecost would have been helpless. Here the Bible as the worker's equipment became also the worker's tool.

The Principle Restated

To re-state, then: we must *know* the Bible by persistent, exhaustive, life-long study. We can never make its precious, life-saving truths too thoroughly a part of our minds and hearts and being. It is the Guide Book to the Way of Life, not only for ourselves, but for those whom we would win. And our work with them is not complete until we have brought them to a recognition of the Bible which shall give it the same unique place in their lives that it has in ours.

But this leading of men to the Bible is to be accomplished, as a rule, by wisely recognizing that those whom we would win to Christ are probably not interested in the Bible to begin with: that their attitude is more likely to be indifferent or even antagonistic to it at the start. This being so, we shall do better to make our approach in the language of their everyday life and in the terms of their present interests, leading them later, with loving skill, to the Book without which any life is sadly incomplete.

Topics and Questions for Study and Discussion

(To test one's grasp of the contents of the chapter)

1. What is, and what is not, the relation of the Bible to the soul-winner?
2. Why is a Bible-quotation seldom the best bait to begin with in seeking to win a soul to Christ?

3. In accordance with what principle must we determine when to use Bible verses?

4. What was Dr. Trumbull's method of personal Bible-study?

5. What was his practise as to quoting Scripture in individual work?

6. What reasons did he give for not using Bible texts?

7. When does the Bible furnish a good meeting-ground of common interest?

8. What were the three difficulties of the young German unbeliever?

9. Describe just how they were met by Dr. Pentecost.

10. State the exceptional features of the young German's case. Show how they made his case different from most cases of every-day opportunity in individual soul-winning.

11. Restate the principle that determines the place of the Bible in individual work.

CONVICTION BETTER THAN
DISCUSSION OR ARGUMENT

(For study before reading this chapter)

1. What is discussion? What is argument? What is conviction?
2. Name some "border-line" questions of conduct concerning which even Christian people disagree.
3. Under what circumstances is it proper for one man to tell another man his duty?
4. What objections can you think of to giving discussion and argument a place in individual work?
5. What is the best way to help a man to decide all border-line questions aright?
6. What characteristic, among the men that you know, seems to give a man the greatest influence with other men? How do you account for this?

VII

CONVICTION BETTER THAN DISCUSSION
OR ARGUMENT

THERE is only One in the universe who can safely tell a man his duty as to the details of everyday life and practise. Therefore it is our chief duty to lead our fellows to that One, and to seek to win them to a loyal acceptance of him as their Head and Guide and Saviour, so that he may settle their questions of duty for them. It is never our duty to attempt to settle for our fellows such questions as God intends they shall refer to him. About the only duty that one man can safely and unconditionally prescribe for another man is the supreme duty of surrender to God's will.

Unwillingness or failure to recognize this simple truth has caused many an earnest worker to become a stumblingblock rather than a guide-post to those whom he honestly longs to help. Many a promising spiritual conversation has gone to pieces on the rock of discussion of details of personal duty. Let us avoid this error as a snare and a pitfall. The Devil will have little to fear from our efforts at individual work if we let them become debates over border-line problems in everyday life.

An actual incident will make the practical application of this truth plainer. A man of the world whom Dr. Trumbull had, after careful study, brought to the point of hearty interest in the claims of Christ, had asked for help in ascertaining the way of salvation.[1]

My companion was different from any one with whom I had ever conversed personally on the theme of themes. He had not been, while a child, under the religious training and influences with which I was most familiar. Hence there seemed to be no such common basis for a preliminary understanding as I had been accustomed to find. Yet this necessitated a coming down to first principles, which, after all, had its decided advantages in such a conference as this.

" My friend, would you like to be saved?" I asked at the start.

" Indeed I would," he replied.

" Do you think that you can save yourself?"

" I certainly do not," was his response.

" Do you know of any Saviour to be trusted except one?"

" I do not," he said heartily.

" Well, now," I said, " there is no necessity of your reading any books on the subject, to learn the way of salvation. [He had asked what books he might read in order to learn more of the subject.] Let me see, here and now, if you are willing to be saved by the one Saviour in his own way. Understand that I do not make any conditions or requirements of conduct or practise, in order for you to be saved; but I will ask you this question, in order to ascertain your attitude toward the whole subject. Suppose that you were to find that Jesus Christ wanted you to refrain from drinking, from smoking, from card-playing, from theater-going, and from much that accompanies these things, would you give them all up, or would you feel that there were some of these things that you could not refrain from?"

My friend thought the matter over with evident seriousness, and then he gave this intelligent answer:

" Well, Mr. Trumbull, there are some of those things that

---

[1] The preliminary part of this case was considered in Chapter V, pages 96-98, of this volume.

I might have different views from yourself about; but if I were convinced that Jesus Christ wanted me to refrain from any one of those things, or from them all, I should be willing to conform my conduct to his wish."

"That's all that I want to know," I said. "I lay down no requirements. I want him who is to be your Saviour to be your guide. Now just go to your room and kneel down before the Lord, and tell him how it is. Tell him that you need a Saviour, that you do not know any Saviour other than himself, and that you want him to save you. Tell him that you are willing to put yourself into his hands, that you will conform your conduct and course to his wishes, and that you want to trust him." [1]

To ask a man to let Christ settle his problems of duty for him is better than to try to settle them for him ourselves. The latter never does any good, and often does great harm. The outcome of the sensible and only safe procedure in this instance was significant. The man became

an earnest, devoted follower of Christ, as I was familiar with him for precious years and in different spheres. He became a close student of the Bible. He and his wife together made an open confession of their new faith, and connected themselves with a prominent church in New York City. They became active in mission-school work, and in that field he devoted his trained business mind to perfecting methods and systems of work, so that he was known widely throughout the country as a leader and guide in that field. He became, after a while, prominent as one of the most influential workers, and director of other workers, in the entire country.

In his personal habits and conduct he became strict and careful, in the line of our talk that evening. [2]

Notice what Horace Bushnell, the famous moulder of theological thought of the middle of the last century,

had to say of the principle of refraining resolutely
from discussing or dictating another man's personal
duty:

> When I, later, told Dr. Bushnell, to whom I had intro-
> duced the young gentleman, of that conversation, and of the
> outcome of it, the good Doctor said, characteristically:
> " That shows how much easier it is to do a big thing than
> a little thing. If you had begun to discuss with this man, at
> that time, any single habit or practise, you might never have
> got beyond it. You would have been stranded on the first
> barrier. But to ask him to trust the whole thing to his
> Saviour, and be guided by him, was the better way. If one is
> right at the center, he is likely to get right at the circum-
> ference." [1]

As with discussion over details of duty, so with
argument over points of belief. Neither discussion nor
argument is likely to draw men closer together; both
tend rather to keep men apart. As such, both are to
be resolutely avoided in a work which seeks above all
else to win others to us, not to keep them at a distance.

But there is a power that we may and must have
in this work, and which utterly outdistances any seeming but empty skill in discussion or power in argument.
It is the power of conviction. That power is well-nigh
irresistible. It will win if anything can. It will swing
a man over from false belief to true unless he is
bound to the false forever.

> A man's *belief* of what he proclaims goes far to make it
> believed by others. So long as he himself has any doubt on
> the subject, he is not likely to convince those who are in
> doubt. This is true in every sphere of life. If a man sees his
> neighbor's house on fire, in the dead of night, his wild, ring-
> ing shriek of "Fire! Fire! Fire! Turn out! Turn out! Your

house is afire!" sounds out on the midnight air with a force that is itself convincing. All who hear it know that the one who utters it feels its truth, and wants others to feel it.

How different it would be if a man should knock timidly at the house door, and say gently that he had reason to think that a fire was kindling in the vicinity, and that he thought it would be well to look into the matter! How could he expect dull sleepers to be aroused on such a call? If his knowledge did not stir him more than this, how could he expect those yet asleep to be aroused from their torpor by him?

Peculiarly is this the case with one who sounds a call to stir a sluggish soul to action, in view of truth that he deems precious and all-important, but which the other is not very anxious about or fully convinced of. Any show of doubt, or indicision, on the part of God's herald, is calculated to shake the confidence of the hearer of the message. This has been found to be the case by every gospel preacher, or winner of single souls, in any sphere. Every show of earnestness, or evidence of intense conviction, on the part of those who stand for Christ, gives added weight to each word of the message from the Captain of our Salvation. Hearty Governor Andrew, of Massachusetts, said of Abraham Lincoln, when he had assumed the presidency, "I'm glad we've got a man who believes something." If a man would have another believe something, he must believe something himself.[1]

Intense conviction, showing itself in intense personality, marks the difference between an ordinary leader, or counselor, and an exceptional one. It was not the number of his soldiers, but his power to use every man as if he were ten men, or a hundred, that made Napoleon, or Phil Sheridan, the general that he was. Surely he who has Christ back of him in his every word and his every deed, ought to feel that he is wielding the power of the Almighty when he acts or speaks for his Saviour in that Saviour's work.[2]

Let our conviction, then, of the truth and joy of our message, shut out argument or discussion forever from our methods in the art of taking men alive. And

---

[1] Pages 177-179.   [2] Page 186.

our conviction may be twofold: the conviction that we know our message is true, and the conviction that the other man knows it is true. This latter, building on the image of God that is in every man, is one of the most disarming attacks we can make against the opposition of unbelief.

Resolute Refusal to Argue

As illustrating the positive effectiveness of conviction, along with a firm refusal to be drawn into a discussion, note the following:

An earnest young clergyman in New England, whom I know well, began his ministry in a parish where his predecessor had lacked strong conviction, and had encouraged, if not cultivated, doubts. The new clergyman's beliefs were startling to his congregation. One Sunday, after the service, a bright young man came up to the minister, and said:

"I don't believe what you are preaching, and I want to discuss your beliefs with you."

"Well, my friend, there's no use in our doing that. I am convinced, and you don't want to be. I am set here to preach the truth that I believe, whether my hearers believe it or not."

Weeks went on. The minister saw his young friend, Sunday after Sunday, in the gallery. One Sunday the minister invited all who wanted to converse with him on the matter of personal religion to come to his study on Monday evening. That evening this young man appeared. Coming up to the pastor's study table, where the pastor sat, he said:

"I am here to-night, not for argument, but for counsel. I've watched you and have heard you for weeks. I know that you have got something that I haven't. Now I want you to tell me how I can get your crucified Christ."

The preacher was ready to help that seeker. And another soul was won to Christ through the counsel of a believer who had convictions.[1]

---

[1] Pages 179-180.

Another worker, whose strength lay not in skilful words but in his simple conviction as to Christ's love and what that love had done for him, had occasion to put this matter to the test.

He was accustomed to ride out from Boston daily to and from a suburban town. One who was frequently his seat-mate was a man prominent as an unbeliever, and who edited a free-thinking periodical. Again and again this man endeavored to draw my friend into discussion on the subject of religion, but without succeeding in so doing. One day my friend openly met the matter in this way:

"I do not want to have a discussion with you on the subject of religion. I'm no match for you in argument. You'd get the better of me every time. But, apart from that, one thing I know, that the Lord Jesus Christ is my Saviour, and I trust him all the time. This is the comfort of my life, and I wish you had the same comfort."

At this his pertinacious seat-mate brought his hand down sharply on his friend's knee and said heartily:

"There you've got me, my friend. I've nothing to offer against that."

My friend's conviction was his best and his resistless argument. "I know whom I have believed" will convince another if anything will. No method of discussion will take its place with any hearer.[1]

And still another instance shows that while a pugnacious unbeliever may be surprised, even startled, by the blunt, insistent putting of an honest disciple's conviction, he is more likely to be won by quiet tenacity here than by intricate argument.

I was in an office where I occasionally had business, and, as I was talking with the proprietor, I said, as he asked my opinion in a matter of principle:

"The Bible says so and so."

[1] Pages 181-182.

"*What* Bible?" he inquired sharply, almost defiantly.

"The Bible," I replied to this question, quietly but firmly.

"Muḥammadans have one Bible. Booddhists have another Bible. Jews have another Bible. Chinese have another Bible. Which Bible do you mean?" he responded.

"*The* Bible," was my response.

"Well, I suppose I know what you mean."

That was a point gained to start with. He admitted that "*The* Bible" was not to be put on a plane with the others, so that he was really in no doubt on the subject.

"But," he added, "I don't agree with you as to the value of the Bible."

"I'm sorry," I replied.

"You think, I suppose," he went on to say, "that the Bible is God's word."

"Of course I do."

"Well, won't you try to prove to me that it is so?"

"No, indeed."

"Wouldn't you like to have me believe the Bible?"

"Of course I should."

"Well, then, why not try to convince me?"[1]

Just here came the answer that startled this polemic would-be disputant out of the ruts of his ordinary and self-satisfied lines of thought. He had asked the "why" of the other's refusal to attempt "logical proof," and he got it:

"*If God has failed in this, with all that he has done for you in a third of a century, I don't propose to set my little hazel-nut brain at the task at this late day.*"

"Why, then, won't you prove to me that God is what you believe him to be?"[2]

To this question there came another answer that must have sunk in deep, not for its arguing power, but by the sheer weight of the immovable conviction that lay back of it:

[1] Pages 182-183.   [2] Page 183.

"The subject is too sacred for ordinary discussion. I wouldn't consent to discuss with you the question whether my mother was really my mother; yet God is dearer to me than is my mother or my father."

At this I left the office without further comment.[1]

That even the unbelieving disputant was ready to recognize the believer's position as a fair one appeared from what followed.

A few weeks later I was there again. He said:

"I understand, Mr. Trumbull, how you feel about the Bible; so I won't ask you to discuss it. But have you any objection to telling me what you understand the Bible to teach on certain points?"

"Not in the slightest," I replied.

Then the way was open for a frank, free, and reverent conference over the teachings of the Bible; and the man who had been a scoffer was ready to be told the truth as to Bible teachings by one who had no doubts on the subject, and who therefore commanded confidence. Several such conferences as this seemed to bring this man into a different attitude toward the Bible and its teachings. After a longer absence than usual from Boston, when I was once more in the office of this man, he said to me:

"Mr. Trumbull, will you tell me just where is your home?"

As I told him, he said:

"I've been very sick. I thought I was going to die, and I wanted to send for you."

Then, as if to show that he had not wholly abandoned his disbelief, he added:

"Not that I was really troubled about myself or my beliefs, but you seem so confident in your beliefs, that, if I was going to die, I wanted you to talk with me."[2]

He was yielding hard; but he was yielding. And it would seem probable that he never would have made

even the reluctant admission that he did to one who
had met him on his own lower ground of debate concerning precious truths that are above and beyond
debate. The opportunity was wider open now than ever
before

for a free talk about Christ and his salvation, which I tried
to improve for that needy soul. "For their rock is not as our
Rock, even our enemies themselves being judges." We surely
ought to be confident in our beliefs, and impress others by
this confidence, as we seek to win them to their Saviour and
ours. We have every advantage, and we should show this in
our loving labor for souls.[1]

Even in that most difficult of all efforts, the winning back to Christ of one who has abandoned his dis-
cipleship, it is conviction that has the power which
argument would utterly lack. The chaplain had cause
to remember this from a war-time encounter.

When first I joined my regiment in North Carolina, I
found there a young lieutenant, whom I had known as an active, earnest Christian worker in his Connecticut home. As
I was looking up the members of my new charge, I called on
him in his tent, and said something of my hope to have his
help in work for my Master.

"No, no, Chaplain," said he, "I've given up all that
stuff. I know now that there's no truth in it, and I don't
want to hear a word on the subject."[2]

How tempted most of us would have been to
"argue that point" with the young backslider! How
much better than argument was this statement of the
chaplain's earnest conviction, coming with somewhat
of the startling unexpectedness of a blow between the
eyes:

"You are not saying now what you believe, Lieutenant."

The braggadocio was all gone as the young fellow asked, in genuine surprise, of a man who had dared to meet his statement of intended conviction with a counter statement whose conviction seemed to ring even truer:

"What do you mean, Chaplain?"

And the earnest, kindly answer came back:

"I mean that I know you well enough to understand that what you said and did, for years, in your faithful Christian work and in your Sunday-school teaching, has not been given up by you out of your inmost heart. You can talk this way to me now, to try to stiffen up your courage of resistance; but when the camp is quiet, and you are alone on your bunk in the darkness, you would never talk in this way to your God, who you know is near you always."

"Well," he said, somewhat more gently, "I don't want to talk about this subject, at any rate."

"But I must talk about it," I said. "It's very real to me. And I'm here because of my belief. I love you too dearly to refrain from speaking to you, and urging you to come back to your old love and faith and duty and joy."

Weeks passed on. When I saw the Lieutenant in his tent I would show him that I, at least, hadn't lost my faith; yet I refrained from provoking any discussion on the subject. He seemed to be grateful for my interest in him, and he never again gave an expression of his unbelief, nor did he say that which would jar on me. I tried to reach him by indirect means, in talking about former interests and persons connected with our work together for our common Master. In this way, at times, the truth we had both then held dear would come into prominence; but no word of unpleasant difference was a result. [1]

It is discussion and argument that bring on un-

[1] Pages 77-79.

pleasant differences, never straightforward, honest conviction. What was the end of this effort in which the believer would admit of no doubt?

After a little there came on a battle in which our regiment lost severely. Several temporary hospitals were opened in small dwelling-houses in different parts of the field of action. As I was occupied in one of these hospitals, I heard that my lieutenant friend lay wounded in another. As soon as I had opportunity, I went over to see him. His right leg had been amputated near the hip. He lay on a cot among many wounded. Looking up as I approached he said cheerily:

" The Lord has got me, Chaplain. I wouldn't serve him with two legs, so he took away one. But now I'll be more of a man with one leg than I was with two."

Then as I spoke warmly of my sympathy with and interest in him, he told of his experience and feelings.

" As my leg went out from under me, and I felt I was gone, I said, 'The Lord's got me, and I'm glad of it.' You were right, Chaplain, that day you came to my tent first, I never really gave up my belief, or had any rest in my life trying to live without faith. And now I believe I shall live nearer the Lord than ever, and have more comfort in him." [1]

It was like that old-time wrestling match at the ford of the Jabbok, when the Lord touched the thigh of a man who had been persistently fighting him, and the rebel was crippled, and the crippling brought a changed life and a new name. Crippled into new life!

The convictions of the chaplain-friend were bearing fruit:

He was confident that he should soon be restored to health, and that he should use his new strength in the Lord's service. I had pleasant interviews with him as he talked of his plans in Christ's service, and he gave convincing evidence of his Christian love and faith. But the shock of the amputation was

[1] Pages 79-80.

severer than he at first supposed, and he soon sank away to his final rest. The prodigal had returned to his loving Father's home. [1]

Topics and Questions for Study and Discussion

(To test one's grasp of the contents of the chapter)

1. What duties can one man safely and unconditionally prescribe for another?
2. What error should we earnestly guard against in doing individual work?
3. What is the best way to help a man to settle his problems of personal life and conduct?
4. What did Bushnell say about center and circumference?
5. What effect are discussion and argument likely to have upon men's relationship to each other?
6. Give your own explanation of why intensity of conviction is such a power in working with men.
7. What two convictions may we have in this work?
8. What is the Christian's best answer to skilled and intricate argument against his belief?
9. When, should you say, is it well to give such blunt answers to men as that of the minister, on page 130 ("I am convinced, and you don't want to be"); or that of Dr. Trumbull, on page 132 ("If God has failed in this," etc.)?
10. Why has our conviction of belief special effectiveness in working with backsliders?

[1] Pages 80-81.

ENCOURAGEMENTS AND INCENTIVES

1. Name the encouragements that you have had from your personal experience in individual soul-winning.
2. Name all the encouragements that you can think of from the experiences and principles so far studied in this volume.
3. What should you say is the greatest incentive we have to the doing of this work?
4. What instances of rebuff by those approached on the subject of personal religion have you known in your own or others' experiences?
5. What prospect of success should you say there is in approaching one who knows beforehand that we intend to seek to win him?
6. Is it a duty, or not, to work with those who are mentally deficient? Describe any instances you have known.
7. Under what circumstances should we expect and urge an immediate decision for Christ?
8. When is our full duty to an individual discharged by a single conversation with that one?

VIII

ENCOURAGEMENTS AND INCENTIVES

I F it is true that there is an abundance of special and
peculiar difficulties in the work of individual soul-
winning, equally true is it that there is a richness of unexpected encouragement and uplift in the work. Every
one who has obeyed the Master's call to make disciples of others can testify to this with a glad heart.
Indeed, the encouragement is so constant, and the re-
wards are so rich, that the wonder is that the Devil
succeeds as well as he does in keeping us faint-hearted!

One of the most frequent experiences that lifts one
up is the unexpected disclosure that God has been
preparing the way for us: that those whom we thought
indifferent or reluctant are eagerly awaiting a word.
This was illustrated by a boarding-house experience
of Dr. Trumbull's:

> For a long time I and my family lived at a boarding-
> house in a New England city. There was, during that period,
> a season of special religious interest, or a general revival, in
> that city. There sat at the same table with us a gentleman
> and his wife, who, as we knew, were not confessing Chris-
> tians, or church-members, and had never expressed to us
> any particular interest in the revival movement in the city.
> One noonday I suggested to my wife that we ought to
> speak to our table neighbors personally on the subject, and
> urge them to surrender themselves to Christ. As she agreed
> with me as to our duty, I proposed that while I would go up
> to the gentleman's place of business and have a loving talk

with him, she should seek out the wife in her room, and
plead with her for Christ. This was agreed to. Then we
knelt together and asked God's blessing on our efforts, and
on those in whose spiritual welfare we were interested.

The gentleman was a bank officer. I called there just after
bank hours, knowing that he would then be disengaged. As I
asked him for an interview, he invited me into the directors'
room, and closed the door. When I spoke of my loving interest in him, and of my purpose in calling, he burst into tears,
and said that he was so glad I had come. Then he told me
how he had longed, day after day, for some one to speak to
him on this subject. When men came in who were prominent
and active in the prayer-meetings, he had tried, in vain, to
lead the conversation to the point of a personal word, but
had always failed. How adroit some Christians are in avoid-
ing the subject of personal religion in business places and in
business hours! I found this man longing to be helped into
the kingdom, and glad to learn the way. That was an ever-
to-be remembered conversation for Christ.

When I went back to the house, at the close of the afternoon, my wife told me, with a cheerful face, of her experience. After my leaving her, as she was preparing to go to
the room of the wife she had on her heart, there was a knock
at her door. As she opened the door that wife came in, and,
bursting into tears, she asked if her friend wouldn't help
her to Christ. She had longed to be spoken to by some one,
and now she could bear this no longer. The two wives went
on their knees together, and they rose with glad and grateful hearts.

That husband and wife soon stood up and confessed
their faith together, as they connected themselves with the
church. They were active for Christ in all the years until
they entered into rest. And their children were prominent
and useful in Christ's service after them.[1]

Two surprises in one day! Two needy souls, eager
and longing for Christ if only some one in Christ
would show the way! Was not the encouragement of

that twofold welcome enough to carry one over some of the hard places in the work?

Even when we are sure that there is little hope of winning a certain person because of that one's known attitude of opposition, we are likely to be encouragingly disappointed if only we will make the trial. Take the difficult case of one who knew beforehand that certain people would endeavor to win him to Christ, and who had no sympathy with the idea.

At one time I passed a Sunday in the home of a superintendent of a village Sunday-school in Connecticut. It was a humble home, back in the country, and no member of the family seemed to have had any special educational advantages. Yet not only the spiritual atmosphere of that home, but its religious exercises and methods, were such as to command my respect, and to make me wish to commend them to others. This led me to ask how all this came about, and, in consequence, I learned this instructive story.

The church of which this man was a member was an ordinary Connecticut church, not given to new things, but keeping on, year after year, in its tried and approved course. But in some way it had been led to try the experiment of having every family in the congregation, or parish, visited by appropriate members of the church for religious conversation. Possibly it was in connection with the labors of an evangelist, but of that I am not sure. My host, who was now the superintendent, was then not a member of the church, nor was any one of his family. He had heard of this proposed movement, and as he sat in his home one day he saw one of the deacons and another church-member drive up to the house and get out for a call. So far from having any special interest in this, he spoke jokingly of it.

But when the deacon was in the home of that man and his wife, speaking with them for Christ as he had never spoken before, they felt the power of his words, and when he knelt with them in prayer they were ready to commit themselves to the Saviour in a sense of need and trust. Their Christian life was started at that time by that individual word to them, as all the sermons and pulpit appeals for years before had not influenced or been felt by them. From that hour that was a Christian household, every child feeling its influence for good. And soon that new comer into the kingdom at middle life was chosen superintendent of the Sunday-school because he was a better man for it than any man who had been trained from childhood in the church.[1]

Suppose the soul-winning deacon had passed by that family because of the " hopelessness " of trying there! He never would have gained the encouragement that must have been his all through the years as he watched the results to that household and to the church and to the whole community from that single appeal for Christ.

Rebuffs Almost Unknown

It is a noteworthy fact that it is a rare, almost an unknown, experience for one to meet a rebuff when courteously and earnestly expressing an interest in another's eternal welfare. Yet this is not strange. Everyone recognizes that the man who seeks to win another to Christ has no " axe to grind," no ulterior motive. There is encouragement here for us all, timid and reluctant as we are. Of his traveling experiences Dr. Trumbull wrote:

I have had hundreds of such conversations with seat-mates on the car, seat-mates whom I had never seen before, and whom I never met again. I never had such a conversation which I had reason to regret, or which seemed to be distasteful to my companion. And many such a conversation has brought out the warmest side of a fellow-Christian.[2]

Similar testimony could be had from every indi-

[1] Pages 147-150.   [2] Page 36.

vidual worker. The biographer of Sir George Williams, founder of the Young Men's Christian Association, writes of him:

> When he crossed the Atlantic he made a point of speaking to every soul on board from the captain to the stoker, from the poker-players in the smoking-room to the emigrants in the steerage. And the remarkable thing is that, although he must have spoken thus of their souls' salvation to tens of thousands, he could never recall a single instance when he received a rude or mocking retort, a splendid tribute to the way in which the world is quick to recognize and appreciate, and pay homage to, true Christian sincerity when accompanied, as it was in the case of George Williams, with the rarest tact and most modest courtesy.[1]

What of the Mentally Deficient?

Is there any gain in working with those who are mentally sub-standard, slow of intellect, or actually half-witted? Are we not doomed to discouragement if we attempt it? Can they appreciate what it is to do right, or to come to Christ? Will not the Lord care for them anyway? Two army experiences gave Dr. Trumbull a conviction as to this field of effort that he never relinquished.

> There were strange characters, as well as strange experiences, encountered in my army Christian work. The army brought all sorts of persons together, and I had to become acquainted with and interested in them all. While at St. Augustine, Florida, in the winter of 1863-64, a part of our regiment did garrison duty at the old Spanish coquina fort, with its bloody memories and its weird legends of former occupants. I was accustomed to hold Sunday-school services each Sunday afternoon, and also mid-week evening

services, in the little chapel opposite the main entrance of the fort. Just outside of that chapel there was a pile of rusty cannon, on which men would sometimes loll while we were having services inside. And as I moved about the fort I had many a talk with men whom I rarely met so familiarly elsewhere.

One day, in walking through the fort, my attention was drawn to a strange face glaring through an iron-barred opening of a dungeon door in the southwestern corner of the casemated walls. It was the most repulsive face I had ever seen. Low-browed, coarse-featured, dark-complexioned, with small black eyes under shaggy eyebrows, and thick sensuous lips, it seemed like a cross between a Digger Indian and a New Zealand native, with the worst peculiarities of both. The expression was one of low cunning, with a mixture of hate and derision. It was an unhuman face, yet the man who bore it was evidently one of my parishioners, or he would not be where he was.

"Who are you, my friend?" I said. "Where do you belong?"

He answered in a low, gruff voice, as if he were resenting an attack.

"I belong to the Tenth Connecticut."

"You belong to the Tenth Connecticut!" I said. "Why, then I'm your chaplain, and I've got an interest in you."

As I kindly questioned the man, I found that he had been most of the time since his enlistment in confinement for insubordination, and therefore I had not met him. After a brief talk I left him. Soon he was released from confinement, and was again with his comrades. I saw him occasionally, and spoke to him kindly, but I did not look upon him as a hopeful case in comparison with others, and had comparatively little to say to him.[1]

Even the chaplain was not beyond feeling the temptation of discouragement in such a case as this. There was a surprise in store for him.

After a while, we left Florida for Virginia. As we moved up along the coast in a crowded transport, this man came to me in the throng, and said softly:

"Misser Chaplin, I want to talk to you."

"Well, I'm always glad to talk to you," I said. "But where can we go to talk? Let us lean over the steamer's rail. That is our only place to talk by ourselves."

As we leaned there together, he told me his strange, pathetic story.

"Misser Chaplin, you 'member when you talked to me at the dungeon door. You spoke kind to me. You said you's my chaplin. I never forget that, Misser Chaplin. I'm a rough feller; I never knowed much. I suppose I'm human, that's about all. I never had no bringin' up. Fust I knowed o' myself I was in the streets o' New Orleans. Never knowed a father or mother. I was kicked about. I came North and 'listed in army. I've had a hard time of it. My cap'n hates the very groun' I tread on."

Then with a chuckle and a leer, as he thought of his Ishmaelitish life, he said: "I *did* worry my cap'n. And he hated me. Ten months with ball and chain! A hard time of it! But what you said at the dungeon door's all true. And what you said in prayer-meetin' is all true."

"Prayer-meeting!" I said. "I never saw you in prayer-meeting."

"No, I was jus' outside, on those old cannon. And now, Misser Chaplin, I want to do right. Misser Chaplin, I suppose we's goin' into a fight, and I want to do my duty. They say I'm a coward. I've never been in a fight, but I want to do my duty." As a friend of mine, to whom I told this story, said, "The only religious instruction this man ever got was through eaves-dropping at a prayer-meeting."

Then in a voice strangely tender in contrast with the first gruff utterance which I heard from him in the dungeon, he said: "Misser Chaplin, you're the only man who ever spoke kind to me. If I get killed I want you to have my money. And if I get killed, won't you have it writ in the paper that Lino died for his country?"

We reached Virginia. We were in a fight. Lino bore himself so bravely that his captain, whom he had worried so

long, called him out before the entire company, at the close
of the engagement, and commended him for his bravery and
good service. Hearing of this, I looked him up after the
fight was over, and congratulated him on his well-doing in
active battle.

"You've done bravely, I hear, Lino, and I'm glad of it."

"Yes," he said, with a softer chuckle than before. "They
called me a coward, but I tried to do my duty. 'Tain't
always the frisky ox that's at the far end of the yoke."

That long friendless man showed, in his way, his intention of doing what God would have him do. Who of us
has better improved his opportunities?[1]

An even more striking encouragement, in the way
of result, came from a tardy recognition of the rights
of those who lack other advantages to a saving knowledge of Jesus Christ.

Among the recruits picked up in Connecticut, for the
sake of the bounty, in the later years of the Civil War, were
some men who would not have been accepted in the army on
their merit. One such man in our regiment was below the
physical standard, and he seemed beneath a fair average of
intelligence. He was a laughing-stock in the regiment. He
was not competent for a soldier's duty. He was unable
to drill. So he was put at a menial duty, and became a
byword and a butt. I do not think that it occurred to me,
at that time, that he was a proper subject for religious conversation. I am speaking of what was, not of what ought
to have been. Possibly the confession of my lack will suggest
to some one else the impropriety of such a failure.

One day, in St. Augustine, as I was walking on the parapet of the old Spanish fort, I came upon this man. No
one else was just then in sight, and it seemed as if it would
be taking nothing from others if I said a word to him. So
I stopped to talk with him. Calling him by his regimental
nickname, I asked:

"Do you ever pray?"

[1] Pages 95-98.

"I say 'Oure Farther,'" was his thick and drawling response.

"Who is your Father?" I asked.

That question he couldn't answer. He had only, by some one, been taught by rote to say the words of that prayer. Then I took him as a little child,—as, indeed, he was a little child in intellect; and I told him of God as his loving Father in heaven, who would be glad to have him pray to him. And I told of Jesus and his love. He listened like a glad child who was taking in a child's lesson, and he seemed to comprehend what I was saying, as well as any of us can comprehend these truths. From that time I had a new interest in that soldier boy, and he seemed to be showing signs of awakened life. He welcomed my interest in him, and he responded gratefully to every word of counsel or suggestion from me. I reproached myself that I had not been readier to estimate him as God estimates every soul whom the Saviour loves and died for.[1]

The immediate response of this needy and neglected child of God to the story of the Father's love had been a surprise and an encouragement to the chaplain. But who but the Father himself could have foreseen the end?

After the war was over I was, one Sunday evening, to make an address in a Connecticut city. As I entered the outer door of the prominent church, a bright-faced young man stepped forward to greet me, calling me by name. As I looked the second time, I saw that it was that anything but hopeful soldier whom I first talked with on the parapet of the old Spanish fort in St. Augustine. On inquiry, I found that he had made a public confession of his faith in one of the prominent churches in that city, and that he was witnessing a good confession. He was a regular attendant in the Sunday-school. As I looked at him, I hoped that I had been of some service to him; for I was sure he had taught me a good lesson,—a lesson that I want to pass on to others. Any soul that Jesus loves is worth our best work in its behalf.[1]

Still another remarkable instance of this kind of work is found in the following experience of a missionary, President Browne of Harpoot College in Turkey:

One evening I was riding into one of our lowest villages in eastern Turkey, and my horse almost stepped upon something in the mire. As I looked, I saw a little humpbacked girl. When she opened her mouth, her utterance was more foul than the mud and mire beneath her. Arriving at the teacher's house, I spoke to him about that little humpbacked girl, and he said: "Don't tell me anything about that girl; she is a lost soul." I worked five days there in that village to persuade the parents of this little girl to allow her to come to our school. Within a year her heart had melted, a character had begun to develop, and her face became bright and hopeful. As the years went by, she developed a marvelous capacity for patience and love, and when from the villages came especially hard cases, we would bring them to her. When she graduated, she was made the principal teacher in our college. She had rare talents for teaching; we had never seen anything like it before. But one day she came to me and said: "I am not contented to be a teacher in the college." "Why not?" I asked. "Why are you not satisfied here?" "I want to go," she replied, "to the places where others do not wish to go." So I sent her out to a place on the northern branch of the Euphrates, where she did a work that none of our teachers had been able to do. She introduced the gospel and founded four churches. Think of it! This "lost soul" had founded four churches, in spite of her deformity and the early influences of her life.

Is Any Opportunity Too Slight ?

There is no such thing as a " trifling " opportunity in the work of soul-winning; no opportunity so slight

[1] Pages 101-102.

that it may safely be passed by as not worth improving. A teacher of a Bible class saw, late one week-day
afternoon in winter, a member of the class hurrying by
his house. The man was going home from his work,
that of a house-painter. The teacher waved a greeting to him through the window, but the man failed to
see it. Thereupon something prompted the teacher
to hurry out of the house, bareheaded, after his friend.
He caught him at the corner, and they stood together
chatting. Upon the teacher's asking the painter how
he had been, he replied that he had had a pretty bad
spell of sickness a few nights before. " I tell you," he
said, " it makes a man think pretty hard when it seems
as though everything was dropping away from him."

" But you're all ready to go whenever you *are*
called, Joe?" asked his teacher with a hearty smile.

" I don't know about that," was the sober answer.
"Sometimes I think I am, and then again I don't
know." This came as a genuine surprise to the
teacher, who had supposed that the man was in no
doubt as to his relation to Christ.

It took but a few minutes' earnest talk there on the
street corner to show this troubled soul that he need
not be in doubt another moment. A meeting with the
pastor was suggested, and gladly agreed to ; and at the
next communion service of the church the painter
stood up and gave public expression to his acceptance
of the Saviour who would have all men ready for his
coming. Would he have been thus ready if that
teacher had felt that his duty was fully discharged in
class on Sundays, or that the casual passing of his
house was too slight an opportunity for a show of
interest.

A personal experience impressed a Christian business man with the measureless gain of counting no opportunity too slight.

He was on his way to an international convention of Young Men's Christian Associations in Montreal. As the train approached that city, a bright young man came into the car as a representative of a prominent hotel in Montreal, seeking guests for his hostelry. My friend inquired as to the location and advantages of the house, in view of the heat of summer, then prevailing. At once the young man waxed eloquent over the subject, and fairly convinced his hearer that this was the place for him.

As my informant arranged for a room there, he asked pleasantly of the zealous advocate:

"My young friend, are you a follower of Jesus?"

"I can't say I am, sir," was the reply.

"Well, if you were in Christ's service, and would plead as earnestly for his cause as you do for the hotel you now represent, you would be a valuable helper to your Master, and you might do a great deal of good to others. I wish you were in Christ's service, using your powers for him."

The young man passed on through the car, and my friend went his way to the city, having simply said this word for his Master, as was his wont. It did not seem to be an exceptionally hopeful occasion, but who can tell?

Several years passed. My friend sat, one day, in his private office in a New England city. As he called out a question to some one in the hallway, his pleasant voice sounded through the building. Almost immediately a strange young man appeared at the office door, and said:

"Excuse me, sir; but, may I ask, did you not attend a convention in Montreal, about the first of July, a few summers ago?"

"Yes, I did, as I well remember; but what of that?"

"Do you remember speaking to a young man on the cars, and telling him you wished he would work for Jesus as faithfully as he was then working for a hotel in Montreal?"

"I think I do, now that you recall it."

"Well, *I* cannot forget it. Your words rang in my ears. They resulted in bringing me into the service of Jesus, and now I am trying to speak words for him wherever I go. Being in this city on business to-day, I came into this building [where were the rooms of the Young Men's Christian Association], and as I was near your door I heard that voice which has been sounding in my memory all these years, and I have come to thank you for what you have done for me."

That delegate to the international convention of Young Men's Christian Associations did more by his word to an individual for Christ than if he had made half a dozen eloquent addresses in the convention.[1]

Bishop C. C. McCabe told of an illustration out of his experience that impressed him with the worth of the opportunity which most of us would consider no opportunity at all:

At one time in a strange city, as the hackman got down from his box and opened the door to let me out, I paid him, and grasping his hand said, "Good-night, I hope to meet you again in glory." I then went into the house, met my host, and retired. About midnight my host knocked at my door and said: "Chaplain, that hackman has come back, and says he has got to see you to-night." When the broad-shouldered, rough-looking man, with whip in hand, was shown up, the tears rolling down his cheeks like rain, he said, "If I meet you in glory, I have got to turn round. I have come to ask you to pray with me."

How mistaken we are when we attempt to measure opportunity by man-made rules!

As John B. Gough said of the one loving word of Joel Stratton that won him: "My friend, it may be a small matter for you to speak the one word for Christ that wins a needy soul—a *small matter to you,* but it is *everything to him."* It is forgetting this truth that causes personal work to be neglected.[1]

How often—or how seldom!—do we think of those who serve us in public places, such as waiters, street-car and railway-train conductors, and sleeping-car porters, as being souls for whom *we* have any responsibility? A prominent Sunday-school leader, W. C. Pearce of Chicago, told the writer of a pleasant surprise he once had when he improved an opportunity that most of us would have counted "too slight." Here is the incident in his own words:

I took the train at the Lake Shore Depot, Chicago, for a town in northern Indiana. I was very tired, and, although it was during the day, I took a seat in the sleeper, and almost before we had left Chicago I was asleep. I had instructed the porter to waken me before I reached my destination; accordingly, as we neared the end of the journey, he came in and aroused me. A few minutes later he returned to brush my clothes and help me with my baggage.

As he was brushing me off I remarked: "My journey ends before yours to-day, doesn't it?"

"Yes, suh," was the answer.

"I wonder which of us will come to the end of the journey of life first?"

"I don't know, suh, I don't like to think about dat, suh."

"Well," said I, "it doesn't matter much if one has a through ticket."

The man looked puzzled, and said, "I don't know what you mean, suh."

Then I explained to him that I had secured a ticket at Chicago, which was nothing more nor less than a promise of a ride, properly signed by the railroad officials. And I pulled from my pocket a small copy of the Bible, and spoke of Christ's free offer of salvation, quoting some one of the promises, and explained that this promise was signed and sealed by the death of Jesus Christ, and that I had accepted that promise and was trusting fully in the journey's ending right.

With a very happy face, which I shall never forget, he responded, "Bless de Lawd, I have that." And he added, "*I have been a porter for many years, but you are the first gentleman that ever spoke to me about Jesus Christ.*"

If, indeed, we let ourselves ever admit that any opportunity may be too trifling to use, we are sure to miss real opportunities that are close by us. It is only by persistent practise in seizing every opportunity that we shall gain the keenness that can see an opportunity where most people would see none. We need not be afraid of seeing too many. For we miss so many! Think of the attitude among Christian people generally that would make such an occurrence as the following possible, among intended ministers of the gospel!

An active worker for individuals was visiting a well-known divinity school in order to have an interview with a student. While waiting for that student he was improving his time, as usual, by seeking individual souls near him. Encountering a janitor, or other helper, in the hall, he had a pleasant, direct talk with him. He found a soul waiting to be helped. He led that soul to the Saviour. In conversation he found that although that soul had been long in the vicinity of embryo preachers, not a word had been spoken to him by one of them. They were waiting to be eloquent to a full congregation. Why should they waste their strength on a single soul? That is an illustrative incident, even if it is not an instructive one.[1]

Those closest to us may be most in need of the personal word for Christ. Only as we carry the commission ever-present in our thoughts, to be obeyed as we go about our daily business, in school or college, in

[1] Page 174.

the home-circle itself, in boarding-house or hotel, on train and boat, have we any assurance against missing priceless opportunities for soul-saving. Our morning prayer should anticipate it as the biggest thing in the day ahead. Our evening prayer should review the day in relation to this. "Lovest thou me? Feed my sheep." [1]

Individual Work Always Needed

For nothing else will ever take the place of individual work in bringing souls into the Kingdom. Without it, some are sure to be missed. Faithfulness in pulpit or Sunday-school class or prayer-meeting are good accompaniments of it, but never substitutes for it. After the Civil War was over the chaplain had occasion to realize this, in his continued efforts both as preacher and individual worker.

A regimental "pioneer corps" did peculiar army service, and its members often exhibited high qualities of courage and daring. They would go before our column to cut a way through forest or bushes, or to construct a bridge or road, sometimes under the enemy's sharp fire. To fill their place and do their work was to win honor and regard from officers and men. They would quickly construct a shelter for an officer, which gave him protection and comfort, as he stopped for a night or a week. In doing this they showed rare skill and taste, and made themselves indispensable to the command as a whole.

Some months after the war I was announced to speak, one Sunday evening, in a prominent church in Western Massachusetts. As I rose in the pulpit I saw in the congregation a well-remembered sergeant in our "pioneer corps." He was one of the bravest of the brave, always prompt and ready in

[1] John 21: 17.

whatever he had to do. Hearing that I was to speak, he had come to listen to his old chaplain. The pastor in whose pulpit I stood told me afterwards that this veteran soldier had a good name in the community, although he was not a church-member. At once I felt that I must reach him for Christ. The chaplain must be faithful that night to the pioneer corps sergeant.

At the close of the service the brave old "pioneer" came forward to give me greeting. After a talk about our campaigning together, I asked him if he wouldn't go with me for a talk to the parsonage, where I was to pass the night. This he was glad to do. By the pastor's consent I had a room where we could be by ourselves. In a free talk with my old comrade, I found him ready and glad to commit himself wholly to Christ. He only needed to know what to do, and to be helped to do it. When I asked him if he was ready and willing to take this step now, he assured me that he was. At this we went on our knees together, and the brave soldier of country became a trustful soldier of Christ. As I knew of him afterwards, I felt that he was one of many who needed only the being enlisted to be ready for active, persistent service.[1]

Yet if the chaplain had let his work cease with his pulpit address that night, the enlistment might never have been made.

The best of prayer-meetings, no matter how well-conducted and spiritual, will never accomplish the work of individually seeking the individual. A young Christian army officer once taught needed lessons in this line.

In each city to which he was assigned he naturally went to the Young Men's Christian Association as a hopeful center and starting-point. There he usually found the weekly prayer-meeting as perhaps the highest point of spiritual devotion. But this was, to his mind, too much after the pattern of an

[1] Pages 105-108.

ordinary church service, where the congregation was largely
of church-members and church-goers, while he wanted to
reach those who were still outside, but who were compelled
to come in, against their ordinary preferences and inclinations.
Hence to this work he vigorously set himself at once.

Going into such a prayer-meeting, early in the evening,
at one time, he asked the leaders how many persons had been
sought out from the highways and byways that evening. On
being told that nothing of the sort had been done, he asked
that all should kneel at once in prayer, offering an ejaculation
of consecration to this service, and of petition for help in this
service, and then all should scatter to the street corners and
drinking-places and gambling-houses, seeking souls, and urging them to come in where they could be helped. Fifteen
minutes or more later they were to return to the Association
rooms, and then they might have a hopeful prayer-meeting
there. The first experiment was an eminent success, and its
every repetition seemed an improvement on this. More of
those for whom they had there hoped and prayed were gathered in in a single evening, under this plan of work, than
under the old plan, or the no plan, in any one year before.

Of course, the good results of this kind of effort were a
surprise to those who had supposed that being willing to pay
for a seat in church, or being willing to look up for themselves
a regular religious service, was an essential preliminary to
being a hopeful member of a regular congregation. This has
been so, in fact, for centuries. In this case gamblers gave up
gambling, drunkards gave up drinking, scoffers gave up scoff-
ing, doubters gave up doubting, and those who had been counted
as outcasts became glad and grateful followers of the Lord
Jesus, urging their old associates to receive life instead of death,
as they had already accepted it. In one instance a rumseller,
influenced by his now rescued customers, abandoned his vile
pursuit and became an active recruiting officer for the Captain of his Salvation. Such results as this are natural when
souls are sought one at a time by one who is in loving, living
earnestness, intent in pursuit of that one soul.[1]

And a young man who had been won to Christ by

[1] Pages 156-159.

the simple word of individual appeal from a stranger wrote in an agony of earnestness:

"O Mr. Trumbull! you cannot urge the followers of Jesus in too strong terms to talk more of him. A kind word may save a soul! That soul may save a thousand! Do they realize it? When I remember, at times, how my soul has longed, when a mere boy, a stranger in a great city, for some one to take an interest in me and my soul's welfare, I feel as though I should fly away for fear there is some one near me smothering the same awful feelings, and longing for that kind word of Christian sympathy.

"I remember very well, the morning I packed my things to go and fill that situation in that city, how my mother prayed for me, and said, as she thought of the temptations I should be subject to, 'O William, how I wish you were a Christian!' I wished so too. She hoped all would be right. When, that day, I went into the garden to say good-by to father, as he saw me coming he turned his head to hide the tears, and he reached out his calloused hand, calloused for me, and said: 'You are going away from home, William, and all you have in this world is your good name. Keep that. Attend church every Sabbath regularly somewhere, and you will come out all right.' I promised him I would. I went away very sad, but determined to keep my promise.

"For one whole year, Sabbath after Sabbath, I attended one church and sat in the same seat, and no one ever intimated that he thought I had a soul; and I was never sufficiently acquainted with a member of the church or congregation to be on speaking terms; yet, at times, my sense of guilt was overwhelming, and oh for a friend!"....

How many souls there are waiting and longing to be blessed, as that Vermont boy waited and longed in his first year away from home! One day, on Broadway, I noticed a crowd about a little child. Pushing in among others, I saw that it was a strayed child. He was lost, and he knew no way of finding himself or his dear ones. Seeing my look of tender sympathetic interest in him, the child looked up, and stretched out his hand to me, saying, in pleading tones, "Won't you please to show me my way home?" That cry

has been sounding in my ears ever since, when I find myself
near a wandering soul like that Vermont boy in the city,
and like others who are about us on every side, as we ride
and as we walk. There is work enough to do for Christ if
only we will help the individuals near us who need our help,
and who are ready to be helped.[1]

Pressing for an Immediate Decision

As to seeing definite results of our efforts in individual soul-winning, that may or may not be our privilege. Our chief concern must be the giving of the
invitation to come to Christ. The results are between
Christ and the individual. Sometimes, perhaps often,
we shall not know what the outcome is. Again, it may
be our duty to press for immediate results, for instant
decision. An illustration of this occurred in one of
Dr. Trumbull's railroad train experiences.

One morning, as I was riding on a train in Western
Connecticut, I saw a young man whom I had seen at a religious meeting the evening before. I had never seen him except at that time; but there was a deep religious interest just
then in the church where I had seen him, and accordingly I
took a seat by his side and began conversation on the subject.
He seemed glad to be spoken to about it, and I said I hoped
he would enter into Christ's service with the others there
who were doing so. He said he wished it were so.

"Then why isn't it so?" I asked. "You have nothing
to do but to commit yourself at once to the loving Saviour
as his servant and follower. He is more ready to accept
you than you are to offer yourself."

"Do you mean, Mr. Trumbull, that here on this car-seat,
just now, I can give myself to the Saviour, and he will accept
me without any further preparation on my part?"

"I mean just that," I said. "The Saviour is ready when
you are. There is no gain in your waiting; and no further

[1] Pages 39-43.

preparation is needed than for you to be ready to give yourself to him and to trust him unhesitatingly."

He said not a word more about himself, but he gave evidence of a loving, trustful soul, when he reached out in thought after another, saying:

"Mr. Trumbull, I've a brother who ought to be a follower of Christ. I wish you could talk to him."

That is one of the first evidences of the Christian spirit and life,—an interest in another soul, and the forgetting of self in that care for another.[1]

Another occasion when the securing of an immediate decision for Christ was a plain duty of the individual worker occurred in an army interview:

One evening, as I was returning to my evening quarters, I saw the gleam of a faint light through a low shelter-tent in our regimental camp. It was long after "Lights Out" had been sounded, and I stooped and scratched at the tent entrance as a signal that I wanted to enter. A call, "Come in," responded, and I crept in. A soldier, seated on the ground, was writing home by a small tallow candle, and I knew that any soldier was in an accessible mood when thinking of his home. So I talked with him about home. A sister, a devoted Christian, was, he said, very dear to him. She had urged him to yield himself to Christ, and he was writing to her that very evening.

I felt that the occasion was a peculiar one, and I must improve it. I urged him to a decision at that very time, and I would not consent that he should postpone it. I saw that all he needed was to come to the act of decision, and there might never be a better moment for this with him than now. So there I remained with him, pleading for Christ until far into the night. I knew that there would probably never be "a more convenient season" than this. And his strong New England mind evidently took in this fact. He was considering the matter well. Finally, he voluntarily knelt with me beneath that shelter-tent, and deliberately consecrated himself to the Saviour's care and service. At this I rejoiced

[1] Pages 36-38.

with him, and thanked my God and his. Then, giving my hand to him, I went on to my quarters with a happier heart.

It was but a little while after this, that, in an engagement in which we had a part, he was killed; and as I said earnest words of prayer over the grave in which we buried him, and as I looked down into his dead face, I was glad that I waited that memorable night until he knelt by my side and gave himself up to his loving and waiting Saviour.[1]

In civil life as well as in war-time we may face opportunities where the duty of pressing for instant decision is a plain one. The following experience made a life-long impression on the one who was privileged, because willing, to be God's representative.

One Sunday I passed with a near relative. There I met a gentleman whom I had never seen before, but who was connected with my relative. I sat with him at the table, and we had pleasant conversation. In the evening this gentleman was out at a church service, and the lady of the house was suffering with a headache. I urged her to retire, while I would sit up and close the house after the visitor came in. As I did this, I sat by the sitting-room fire, on the cold winter night. When the visitor was in, and the house was closed, we still sat together there.

He spoke of the service that he had attended, and he was evidently much impressed by the sermon.

"You don't often hear a sermon like that, especially from such a minister," he said. "The minister brought us right up face to face with the Judgment Seat, and there he left us. There were no soft words to ease us down, such as, 'But I trust this is not for you, my brethren.'"

Then, as if soliloquizing, as he sat there looking into the fire, he added:

"*I tell you that, in the great day, we who go over to the left hand will not feel very kindly toward the men who have glossed this thing over, when they had a chance to tell us the plain truth.*"

[1] Pages 89-91.

The impressed man was much older than myself, old enough, perhaps, to be my father; but he had been brought to my side in a condition of mind to need help; and I was there to speak for Jesus. It was not a question of seniority, nor of long acquaintance, to be considered by one who represented the Eternal. Laying my hand lovingly on his knee, as he sat by my side looking thoughtfully into the fire, I said:

"My friend, what do you mean by speaking of 'we who go over to the left hand'? You belong on the right hand, and you ought to recognize this. The judge is your Saviour. You ought to trust him fully as such."

"I suppose I ought to," he responded.

"Well, do you not?"

"I can't say I do."

At this I drew my chair around so that I could look directly into his face, and I said earnestly, feeling the full force of my words:

"This is God's doing, and you must recognize it. God has brought us to this house to meet for the first time in our lives. He has planned it so that you should go out to that evening service, and hear that impressive appeal. And now, while all others in the house are asleep, you and I sit here facing the question of questions for your soul. I cannot leave you until you settle it. I speak for the Saviour when I urge you to commit yourself to him for now and forevermore."

Then, reaching out my hand, I said:

"My friend, you realize what all this means, and its importance. Now, promise me that this night, before you sleep, you will, on your knees, tell your loving, longing, waiting Saviour, that you've delayed this thing altogether too long, but that you won't do so any longer. Tell him that you trust him because he is the Saviour, and you are one whom he wants to save. Give me your hand on this, my friend, and then go to your room and do what you know to be your duty."

My companion evidently felt that it was a crisis hour with him, and he could not evade the sense of this. My hand was outstretched to him. For some time he said not a word, but I saw he was quivering with intense emotion. Meanwhile I was praying in my heart for a blessing on him in his conflict of soul. Then, with a convulsive movement that shook his

strong frame, he put out his right hand and clasped mine as
though it were for life. I realized that he had given himself
to his Saviour. Rising, I asked God's blessing on him, and
bade him good-night, and we parted. I went to my room for
the night, and to pray for him, and he went to his room to
pray for himself.

Before he came downstairs in the morning I left for my
home. I never saw him again. Before the day closed he left
that house for his home. By a severe railroad accident, on
his way home, he was fatally injured, and soon he was with
the Saviour to whom he had trusted himself.[1]

Of one thing we may be sure, and we must make
this unmistakably plain to those whom we would win:
Jesus Christ *accepts at once*. If there is any delay, it
is not of Christ's causing. This truth is not so com-
monly understood as we might suppose. Its need is
illustrated in a case already considered.[2]

When I met him the next morning I asked him if he had
done as he promised to. As he said that he had, I inquired
if he felt that the Saviour had accepted him.

"I don't suppose that he has yet," was his reply.

"Why not?" I inquired.

"I don't suppose that Jesus Christ would accept me at
once," he said.

"Well, then the responsibility is with him. I don't see that
you have anything more to do about it," was my reply.

"What do you mean?" he asked, with a surprised look.

"Why, if you have gone to the only Saviour there is, and
have offered yourself to him, telling him you are willing to
shape your course by his directions, and he is not ready to
accept you, but wants to wait a while, there seems to be nothing else for you to do."

"Do you mean," he asked, "that I ought to believe that
Jesus Christ at once accepts me, and that I can fully trust
him now as my Saviour?"

---

[1] Pages 67-71.

[2] In Chapter VII, pages 125-128, of this volume.

"That certainly is the way I understand it," I said. "I
can't see any other way. It seems to be that or nothing."

"Then I'll do that," he said earnestly, and he evidently
meant what he said.[1]

Vital Importance of Follow-Up Work

We certainly have a responsibility to work for results just so long as the result does not appear in one
who is still within our range of influence. The need
and duty of "follow-up" work here are as vital as
in every other field of effort. Our failure to follow up
a preliminary endeavor, which was good as far as it
went, may mean complete failure so far as that soul
is concerned. Yet how few are willing to be as persistent as was a student of whom Henry Drummond
told?—here is the story in Drummond's own words:

One night I got a letter from one of the students of the
University of Edinburgh, page after page of agnosticism and
atheism. I went over to see him, and spent a whole afternoon
with him, and did not make the slightest impression. At
Edinburgh University we have a Students' Evangelistic Meeting on Sunday nights, at which there are eight hundred or one
thousand men present. A few nights after this, I saw that
man in the meeting, and next to him sat another man whom I
had seen occasionally at the meetings. I did not know his
[the latter's] name, but I wanted to find out more about my
skeptic, so when the meeting was over, I went up to him and
said, "Do you happen to know ——?"

"Yes," he replied, "it is he that has brought me to Edinburgh."

"Are you an old friend?" I asked.

" I am an American, a graduate of an American University," he said. "After I had finished there I wanted to take
a post-graduate course, and finally decided to come to Edinburgh. In the dissecting-room I happened to be placed next

[1] Pages 64-65.

to ——, and I took a singular liking for him. I found out that he was a man of very remarkable ability, though not a religious man, and I thought I might be able to do something for him. A year passed and he was just where I found him."

He [the skeptic] certainly was blind enough, because it was only two or three weeks before that that he wrote me that letter. "I think you said," I resumed, "that you only came here to take a year of the post-graduate course."

"Well," he said, "I packed my trunks to go home, and I thought of this friend, and I wondered whether a year of my life would be better spent to go and start in my profession in America, or to stay in Edinburgh and try to win that one man for Christ, and I stayed."

"Well," I said, "my dear fellow, it will pay you; you will get that man."

"Two or three months passed, and it came to the last night of our meetings. We have men in Edinburgh from every part of the world. Every year, five or six hundred of them go out never to meet again, and in our religious work we get very close to one another, and on the last night of the year we sit down together in our common hall to the Lord's Supper. This is entirely a students' meeting. On that night we get in the members of the Theological Faculty, so that things may be done decently and in order. Hundreds of men are there, the cream of the youth of the world, sitting down at the Lord's table. Many of them are not members of the Church, but are there for the first time pledging themselves to become members of the Kingdom of God. I saw —— sitting down and handing the communion cup to his American friend. He had got his man. A week after he was back in his own country. I do not know his name. . . . He was a subject of Christ's kingdom, doing His work in silence and in humility. A few weeks passed and —— came to see me. I said, "What do you come here for?"

He said, "I want to tell you I am going to be a medical missionary."

It was worth a year, was it not? [1]

[1] From "The Life of Henry Drummond," by George Adam Smith, pages 364-366.

Sometimes we may be surprised to find that one is
confidently expecting to be followed up, and would
lose faith in us if we disappointed him. An illustration of the importance of this kind of " follow-up "
work is found in the following experience of Dr.
Trumbull's:

> On one occasion, I met, in civil life, a fellow-officer, whom
> I honored and looked up to. In a strange place, we were in
> crowded quarters, where there was not a separate bed for
> each. In consequence, we two, who had slept on the field
> under the same blanket, shared the same hotel bed. Our
> army experiences made each of us more willing to consent to
> this arrangement than if we had not been in the army. My
> kneeling in prayer, before I lay down, opened the way for a
> close and loving talk on the precious relations which are
> between those who are one in Christ,—a union closer than
> that of fellow-soldiers.
>
> My officer friend, although reverent toward Christ and his
> salvation, was not ready to express his personal trust in the
> Saviour. As I tenderly urged him to commit himself to the
> one Saviour, he confessed that he was not ready to do so, be-
> cause of a reason that he deemed sufficient. As we con-
> versed that night on the subject, he told me that if a certain
> state of things should ever exist, he would be ready to take
> the step, as he was not now. That night's conversation and
> my officer friend's conditional promise were stored in my mind,
> and he was a subject of my prayers.
>
> As the months passed on, the state of things which he
> suggested as likely to change his view as to his personal duty
> came about. When I knew of this change in affairs, I had his
> promise in mind, and in the early morning I presented myself
> at his home.
>
> " I told my wife that the chaplain would be up here to
> see me, after this," was the greeting that he gave me, as I
> entered his home. *What if I had failed to remember my
> promise at a time like this?*
>
> That brave officer was ready to do his duty. He openly
> took a stand for Christ. His influence over others was great.

He became known throughout the land as a Christian. If I had never been the means of winning any other to a confession of the Saviour, I should feel that all my labors with individuals were more than repaid by the result of that one evening's talk with this soldier of country and of Christ.[1]

We must labor as though the whole responsibility for another's eternal choice rested upon us, while we rejoice in the knowledge that it is not we alone that work, " for it is God who worketh in you both to will and to work, for his good pleasure."[2]

Topics and Questions for Study and Discussion

(To test one's grasp of the contents of the chapter)

1. What is one of the most frequent of the encouragements in this work?
2. Why is no case ever hopeless?
3. Why are rebuffs in this work so rare?
4. Why are the mentally deficient even more likely than others to respond to the individual appeal?
5. What reason did John B. Gough give why no opportunity is too slight?
6. Why ought we really to be thinking more about the "trifling" opportunities than about the obviously greater ones?
7. Why is it that the preaching service and the prayer-meeting can never take the place of individual work in winning souls?
8. When is it a duty to expect and work for an immediate result?
9. What vital truth must we make plain to those whom we would win, as to the time of Christ's acceptance?
10. When have we a duty to do " follow-up " work?

[1] Pages 108-110.   [2] Philippians 2: 13.

HOW OUR LORD WORKED

(For study before reading this chapter)

1. Which is the more important question for Christians to answer: "What would Jesus do?" or, "What would Jesus have me do?" Why?

2. How far have we reason to believe that Christ would do to-day, if he were a man on earth, as he did nineteen centuries ago?

3. What instances can you recall of Christ's individual work?

4. Upon which should you say the emphasis of Christ's teaching lay: death, or life? Give Gospel passages in proof.

5. Under what circumstances did Christ criticize or condemn men? Cite instances.

6. What principles of individual work, as ascertained in these studies, are illustrated in Christ's work on earth? Cite an instance that illustrates each principle.

IX

HOW OUR LORD WORKED

I T is a truth often missed that, while we have work to
do *for* Christ, we have not Christ's work to do. He
did many things, some of which we ought not to do,
others of which we could not do if we would. It is
important to bear this in mind as we make a study of
any part of our Lord's work. We are not Messiahs.
We are not Saviours. We are not to seek to imitate
the details of all that the Messiah and Saviour did.
But we are his messengers and representatives, and we
must work in accordance with his principles.

Let us now test the principles that we have already
found to be important in soul-winning, by ascertaining whether they seem to have the confirmation of
Christ's own practise and teachings.

The Individual in First Place

That the winning of and caring for the individual
soul is the most important work in the Kingdom, given
preferred place by Christ for himself and for ourselves,
we have already seen in our recognition of the place
of the paradox in the Way of Life.[1] Christ's teaching as to this is unmistakable. Seven of the eleven
apostles who remained true to him were won by the
personal appeal to them as individuals[2]; and probably

John
I : 35-5;
Matt. 9 : 9
Mark
I : 19, 20

[1] See pages 31, 32 of this volume.   [2] See page 36 of this volume.

the other four were,—the circumstances of their win-
Matt. ning are not recorded. Again, the ninety and nine are
18 : 12, 13; to be left in order to seek and find the one lost. In
25 : 31-46 the picture of the judgment one's eternal life or death
is determined by the test of having ministered "unto
one of these my brethren, even these least." On the
evening before his crucifixion, alone in the upper room
with his trusted eleven friends, Jesus prayed to the
Father in joyous acknowledgment of the completion
John of the work for which he had lived: "These [my
17 : 25, 26 disciples] knew that thou didst send me; and I made
known unto them thy name, and will make it known;
that the love wherewith thou lovedst me may be in
them, and I in them." He was not thinking now of
the multitudes that he had addressed, but of the little
group of individuals that he had won; his life-work
was a success because these few had been won. And
the work for which he had come, and in which he had
thus succeeded, was the work which he committed, for
its continuance, to them and to us: "and bear ye also
John witness, because ye have been with me." "As the
15 : 27, Father hath sent me, even so send I you." "Ye are
margin; my friends, if ye do the things which I command you."
20 : 21;
15 : 14; The cry of the individual rang louder and carried
Mark more weight with our Lord than the word of the
10 : 46-52 crowd. Jesus turned from the many to ascertain the
need of one, and to meet that need.

A Mission of Winning, Not of Opposing

Christ's mission was to win men to him, not to
drive them from him. He came not to tell chiefly
about sin and death, but about salvation and life. To
dwell on the dark side drives men from us; to dwell

on the bright side draws them to us, if they can be won at all. And we find the emphasis of the Gospels unmistakable on this point. " In him was life; and the life was the light of men.... There was the true light, even the light which lighteth every man, coming into the world." " For God sent not the Son into the world to judge the world; but that the world should be saved through him." " The Father that sent me, he hath given me a commandment, what I should say, and what I should speak. And I know that his commandment is life eternal."

John
1 : 4, 9

John
3 : 17

John
12 : 49, 5c

Not only was the whole purpose and mission of Jesus Christ to win men, but his method of revealing his mission was to use a bait that would win at the start, if possible. He did this by the use of the two kinds of bait the value of which we have already seen: commending the good in men, rather than criticizing the evil; and giving their present interests prominent place to begin with.

Beginning With Men's Present Interests

One of the most memorable instances of Christ's recognition of men's temporal interests as a first step in winning them to him was that of the first miraculous draught of fishes and the call of the fisherman, already fully considered.[1]   But his resolute attention to men's temporal interests was characteristic of his entire ministry. Not only by his miracles of wholesale healing and feeding did he show this, but in numerous individual ministries as well.

Luke
5 : 1-11

With the sinful woman of Samaria who had come

---

[1] Chapter IV, pages 75-78, of this volume.

John to draw water from the well of Jacob, he commenced
4:5-26 with a request for a drink of water, and from that
starting point of *her* interest he led her lovingly, skil-
fully, without any direct condemnation of her great sin,
to the point where she was ready to confess her sin,
to believe in his declaration of Messiahship, and to
bring a whole city under his influence.

John   With Nicodemus, a trained and scholarly Pharisee
3:1-21 whose chief interest was the rabbinical study of the
Kingdom of God, and the Jews' place in that Kingdom,
Jesus needed to use no indirect means at all, but,
seizing at once upon that which interested Nicodemus
most, he revealed to him his own ignorance of the
Kingdom, and his need of that which Christ alone could
offer. The power of conviction rather than argument comes out in verse 11: "we speak that which
we know, and bear witness of that which we have
seen."

John   The absorbing interest of the man helpless for
5:2-14 thirty-eight years was his physical need; with that
interest the Great Physician began, and led from it to a
spiritual, life-bringing word.

John   With the multitude that had been miraculously fed,
:25-35 Jesus went at once to the shallow bottom of their interest,—more bread,—and held them absorbed until
he could tell them of the true bread out of heaven,
and to their cry, "Lord, evermore give us this bread,"
could answer with the Good News: "I am the bread
of life: he that cometh to me shall not hunger, and
he that believeth on me shall never thirst."

When Jesus went to Jerusalem to attend the Feast
of Tabernacles, and wanted to let his mission be
known there at the center of Judaism, he worked in

accordance with this same principle. "On each of its John
[the feast's] seven days a procession following a priest 7 : 37, 38
wound down the side of the temple hill to the pool of
Siloam, the priest bearing a golden vessel which was
filled with water at the pool. It was borne back to
the temple, and poured forth, while the joyous crowd
chanted the ancient words, 'With joy shall ye draw
water from the wells of salvation.'" Was it strange
that the audience was held with a tremendous thrill
when, "on the last day, the great day of the feast,
Jesus stood and cried, saying, If any man thirst, let
him come unto me and drink"?

Again, when he wanted to challenge the attention John
of the Jews, who, though under galling subjection to 8 : 31-36
the earthly power of Rome, prided themselves on being
intellectually and morally the freest people in the
world, he proclaimed that if they would turn to him
and abide in him, they should be made free!

When a heart-broken sister ran to meet him to tell
him of her brother's death, his first word to her was
to remind her lovingly of the resurrection in which
she believed. From that he could tell her in Whom
was the hope of the resurrection for all, and it was John
not difficult to bring her to the confession: "thou art 11 : 18-27
the Christ, the Son of God."

Always did Jesus seem to connect himself intimately with the interest of the person whom he hoped
to help. When one of his own disciples, to whom
he promised that they should follow him where he was
going, complained that they did not know the way, at
once came the answer: "I am the way." When that John
same disciple later showed that his chief interest was 14 : 1-6;
honest doubt over the resurrection story of the others, 20 : 24-2

Jesus unhesitatingly met the doubter just where he
was, and dispelled the doubt.

This principle of beginning with men's temporal
interests, which our Lord made so prominent in his
own work, he laid upon his disciple-representatives as
Matt. he sent them forth to work for him. They were to
10 : 8 heal, cleanse, and bring to life, as part of their intro-
duction to those whom they would reach for Christ.

Commending, Rather than Condemning

The other bait-principle that we have studied, the
use of hearty commendation, is prominent in Christ's
earthly ministry. The surest way to drive men from
us is to begin with condemnation or criticism. It is
not reasonable to suppose that we can win men to ourselves or to Christ if we begin by telling them of
their sins. Christ did not work that way. He never
began his message to any individual or groups of persons by condemnation of sin. He did not hesitate to
denounce sin and sinful persons under certain circumstances, as when his proffered salvation had been re-
Matt. jected or was being actively opposed; or when religious
1 : 20-24; leaders who posed as God's representatives misrepre-
12 : 24-37 sented God and attacked Jesus Christ as from the
Mark Devil; or when he was answering an attack of
7 : 1-13 criticism by vigorous, unanswerable counter-criticism;
Matt.
17 : 19-21 or when he chided his own disciples for certain failures
Mark after they had been won to him. But when Jesus set
16 : 14 out to win a person to himself, it seemed to be his
resolute purpose to find something in that one which
he could commend, and then to commend it in all
heartiness.

For example, the men whom Jesus first invited to

follow him undoubtedly had as glaring sins and as obvious defects as most of us have to-day. Those imperfections must have been quite as much of a trial to Jesus as our fellows' shortcomings are to us. But he did not commence by telling them of this, nor did he seek to help them at the outset by showing them what was wrong with them. His first recorded word to faulty Simon was, " Thou art Simon the son of John: John 1:4 thou shalt be called Rock," as though to say, " for you deserve a stalwart name." So with another of the disciples: there is no reason to suppose that Jesus could not have found, and did not see, any sin in Nathanael; but instead of condemning that which was there, Jesus' first word was in outspoken, hearty admiration of this John 1:4 man, in that he was particularly free from craftiness, or deceit.

The Gospels do not record our Lord's first words to each of the twelve, but it is reasonable to believe that this method of approach was his method with them all, not excepting Judas Iscariot. Even apocryphal tradition preserves the deliberate intention of Christ to see the good in others, when it tells of a dead dog lying by the roadside, kicked aside and scorned by priest and Levite, until Jesus of Nazareth, passing by, looked at the little animal and said gently, " His teeth are very white."

We must learn to work in that way, if we would take men alive as Christ did. We shall never lose, but always gain, in our influence for Christ, if we determinedly seek that which can be commended in one whom we would win, and speak heartily of it.

Christ's singling out of Zacchæus, a man in whom there was evidently little that was likable, for the honor

Luke
19 : 1-10   of a visit, with the confidence in the man's best side which that implied; the entire absence of any word of criticism by Christ of the much in the man's life that was open to criticism; the triumphant outburst of the man's higher nature as the result of this unexpected kind of treatment; and our Lord's hearty word of commendation closing the incident: could there be a plainer example of our Lord's endorsement of this principle of approval and commendation in soul-winning?

That scribe to whom Jesus said, after they had talked together about love as better than burnt offerings, " Thou art not far from the kingdom of God,"

Mark
12 : 28-34   must have had a quickened sense of the power and saving work of the young Teacher from Nazareth.

Over and over again Jesus strengthened faith by recognizing or commending faith. The tiny, mustard seed grain of faith that was hardly alive had, in many a soul, its first sprouting toward vigorous life because of our Lord's willingness to commend what others would have thought beneath commendation. Or again, when faith in him was already strong, he did not hesitate to render a tribute to its nobleness which must

Matt.
8 : 5-13;
9 : 20-22;
9 : 27-29;
15 : 21-28
Mark
10 : 46-52
Luke
7 : 36-50;
17 : 11-19
  have led it on to still deeper possibilities. Study the cases of the centurion of Capernaum, the woman who touched Christ's garment in the crowd, the two blind men, the Canaanitish (Syro-Phœnician) woman, Bartimæus the blind beggar, the sinful woman at the house of Simon the Pharisee, the grateful leper of the border of Samaria.

Christ's instructions to his disciples, both the Twelve and the Seventy, were plain here also. They were to enter upon a mission primarily of winning

men, not of condemning or denouncing. Their first
word to any house into which they might enter was
to be a salutation of peace. Only after they should
be met by actual opposition were they to utter any
word of disapproval.

Matt.
10 : 11-16
Luke
10 : 3-11

Other Principles of Our Lord's Work

Jesus sought to find points of agreement with those
whom he would win,—therefore a fundamental principle in this work. To those to whom the law and the
prophets were vital matters of religion and conduct
he said, " Think not that I came to destroy the law or
the prophets: I came not to destroy, but to fulfil."
And he enlarged upon this until there was no room
for any honest doubt of his meaning.

Matt.
5 : 17-19

He led his followers to think most about what
they *believed,* not what they were in doubt about,—
another cardinal principle of success in soul-winning.

Matt.
16 : 13-20
John
9 : 35-38;
11 : 25-27

He refused to offer "proof" to those who, he
knew, had no honest desire for proof nor any wish
to believe in him or to ascertain the truth. Yet he
was ready to furnish proof to one who *wanted* to
believe.

Matt.
12 : 38, 39
16 : 1-4
John
20 : 25-27

As for the place of Scripture-quoting in soul-
winning, we shall find, as we review these instances of
our Lord's work, that the principle considered in
Chapter VI would seem to have Christ's endorsement.
If the Scriptures were prominent in the interest of
those whom he addressed, he recognized that interest
by quoting Scripture. But if some other interest was
more prominent in the immediate life of the one with
whom he dealt, that other interest was given prior
place at the outset.

Always his enduring purpose seemed to be to convince men and women that they were dear to Him and to the Father just as they stood: faulty, sinning, unworthy, discouraged or hopeful, it mattered not if they would but let Him come close alongside.

Topics and Questions for Study and Discussion

(To test one's grasp of the contents of the chapter)

1. What is the difference between doing Christ's work, and doing work for Christ?
2. Mention your reasons for believing that our Lord gave preferred place to individual soul-winning in his own work, and that he would have us do so to-day.
3. Quote passages to show that Jesus came to point out the way of life, rather to condemn unto death.
4. What two kinds of bait, in the winning of men to himself, were prominent in Jesus' work?
5. Cite instances of Jesus' use of men's present interests as bait.
6. What reason have we to believe that he specifically instructed his disciples to use the bait of men's present interests?
7. When did our Lord criticize and denounce?
8. Cite instances of his use of commendation as bait.
9. Cite instances of his use of commendation in building character or strengthening faith.
10. What shows that Christ's disciples were instructed to win at the start rather than to denounce?
11. Mention other principles of our Lord's work which should be controlling principles of our own.
12. Find your own illustrations of our Lord's use, or non-use, of Scripture passages, and ascertain whether the principle formulated in Chapter VI would seem to have the approval of his example.
13. State the enduring purpose of Jesus' life-time ministry.

THE PRINCIPLES REVIEWED

1. What principles of successful soul-winning stand out most clearly in your mind, as the result of these studies?

2. What would you say are likely to be one's greatest encouragements in the work?

3. What are the chief incentives to doing the work?

4. What are the chief difficulties in the work?

5. Why may we properly call the work of individual soul-winning an art?

6. To what facts and factors do you attribute the superior effectiveness of individual work?

X

THE PRINCIPLES REVIEWED

IF we do not learn and practise the art of taking men alive, we shall be failures in the chief work of Christ's Kingdom on earth. In entering upon the work, we recognize three distinctive truths:

1. The work of individual soul-winning is the greatest work that God permits men to do.

2. It was Christ's own preferred method of work, as it is his preferred method for us to-day. For it is always the most effective way of working.

3. It is the hardest work in the world to do, and it always will be the hardest.

But it is an art of well-defined and plainly-recognizable principles, which any one may learn who is willing to pay the price in study and practise, and in which laymen and ministers are on an equal footing. There is no professional point of vantage here.

That individual soul-winning is the greatest work is part of the paradox-principle of the Way of Life. One is more than many. The least is the greatest. You cannot reach a thousand unless you can reach one. The greatest preaching is the preaching to an individual. The greatest preachers, pastors, evangelists, and missionaries agree as to this. General preaching is preliminary or preparatory to this end and climax of effort, individual work for individuals.

The three points proved

183

That it was Christ's preferred method in his earthly ministry is seen from a study of the Gospels and an examination of the relative results of his individual and his general work. Seven of the eleven faithful apostles were so won; so also was the last of the apostles, Paul. That it is Christ's preferred method for us to-day is seen from the easily proved superior effectiveness of the method in every branch of religious and secular life.

That it is the hardest work, is inevitable. Because it is the most effective sort of warfare against the Devil, it is the kind of effort which the Devil most bitterly opposes, seeking always to persuade us away from it by the subtle, poisonous suggestion that we may harm the cause of Christ if we attempt it just now. For this reason it will never grow easy. Nor ought it to; its costliness is a secret of its effectiveness, and when it is easily done there is grave question whether it is effectively done.

What the work demands   The obligation to do this work rests with equal weight upon every confessed follower of Christ. Failure here is open disloyalty to the Commission.

Individual work is simply a telling others of our experience of Christ's love, so that they may share it. Efficiency in this does not demand an expert knowledge of the Bible or of theology, nor skill and power in argument and discussion. It does call for unshaken knowledge of what Jesus Christ has done for us, and a deeply-rooted purpose to share that knowledge with others. We must know Christ, and we must know the one to whom we would make Christ attractive.

The best way to begin in this work is to begin; the best time to begin is now. The only mistake we need really to fear is the mistake of holding off. There are few errors to dread *in* the work; the great error is the error of keeping out of the work.

Our feelings must not be recognized as factors at all. Their presence or absence is to be brushed aside, ignored. Feeling like it is not the secret of success in this work; will-power, resolute intention persistently carried out, is the secret. We must and we may love those whom we do not like. *Unimpo tance ot our feel ings and short coming*

Our own personal shortcomings must not deter us. What Christ is, not what we are, is our message. We speak as saved sinners, not as superior beings. Yet the doing of this work is bound to have a powerfully uplifting influence upon the personal life and character of those who engage in it.

A life-resolve that every Christian worker ought to consider is the following: "Whenever I am in such intimacy with a soul as to be justified in choosing my subject of conversation, the theme of themes shall have prominence between us, so that I may learn his need, and, if possible, meet it." Notice that this basis for one's efforts shuts out indiscriminate, haphazard efforts, such as approaching utter strangers with an inquiry concerning their souls; conforms to the usual and proper courtesies and conventionalities of life; respects a man's individuality; but recognizes the theme of themes as worthy of a place in any conversation which one has the right to direct. *The life. resolve*

As we are face to face with an opportunity, our whole attention should be centered upon the person whom we would win,—nothing else. We must seek to know him in order to know his interests; having learned what his interests are, we must begin by work- *Two baits : present interests. honest commen dation*

ing with them just as they are, not as we think they
ought to be. This is the secret of tact: a touch in
keeping with, rather than apart from, our man's present interests. That which we put forward, in line
with his present interests, to catch his attention and
win him to us, is bait. Bait is a prime essential in
winning men to us. The first miraculous draught of
fishes is one of the striking instances of our Lord's
use of this kind of bait in winning men to him.

Another effective kind of bait, always available,
is honest commendation. One reason for its effectiveness is its rarity. Criticism and denunciation, no matter how glaring the other's shortcomings may be, have
no place in soul-*winning*. Denunciation does not win,
it antagonizes. Our business as soul-winners is to
draw men to us, not to drive them away. Genuine,
outspoken commendation always wins.

Seeking common interests   Salvation may sometimes be made attractive to men
by showing that it is just as important in this world
as in the next,—indeed, that its chief value to human
beings while they are human is its present value. This
will be a new thought to many who have had mistaken, stereotyped ideas of Christian truth. But it is
in line with their present interests, which are the only
interests we have to work with.

It is important to make the way of salvation simple.
"Faith is that act by which one person, a sinner,
commits himself to another person, a Saviour."

It is often costly work to seek and find and become
deeply interested in another man's interests; but it is
always possible to do this. The question is not, "Am
I naturally interested in this one and his interests?"
but, "Am I willing to *get* interested?" We can always

get interested if we are willing to pay the price in time and effort. And the deliberate cultivating of another's interests is sure to break down opposition and win that one if persisted in.

Differences of denominational or other religious belief are never sufficient to keep two men from finding common ground, if only one of the two is determined that they shall. There are certain fundamental agreements of belief which can always be found to build upon if one resolutely seeks points of agreement rather than of difference.

We may properly identify ourselves with any interest of another's provided the doing so does not demand a lowering of one's own standards of right and duty. We must often go " far afield "; we need never " let down."

Only Christ can safely settle questions of duty for men. One man can never settle them for another, and ought not to attempt it. Therefore discussions as to details of one's personal life or duty are to be resolutely barred out of our conversation in individual soul-winning. Failure to hold to this principle may defeat our most earnest attempts to reach others. It is our duty simply to lead men to the Saviour who will be their Guide, and insist that they let Him alone tell them their further duty. " If one is right at the center, he is likely to get right at the circumference."

Conviction, not discussion or argument

Conviction as to the truth and the joy of our message—a conviction that only our own personal experience can give—is our greatest strength in this work. It is to take the place of all argument and discussion, for it is all-powerful while they are worse than weak. Men are never argued into the Kingdom of Heaven; they are often estranged from God and man by argument. But men are constantly won over to belief in, and loyalty to, the Saviour, by the magnetism of the irresistible conviction of a man whose belief is beyond and above and better than argument. Our conviction may safely be twofold: conviction, of course, that what we believe is true; and conviction that the man whom we are trying to win knows it is true, no matter what he professes. For every man is made in God's image.

Place of the Bible   Because the great majority of persons who need to be brought to Christ are not specially interested in the Bible, therefore Bible verses are not likely to be the best bait, at the outset, for winning souls. The Bible does not, as a rule, offer common meeting-ground to begin with. A Bible text is not attractive to most of those who need our help. The fact that it ought to be has nothing to do with the case. We must work with men as they are, not as they ought to be.

But the Bible is the soul-winner's indispensable equipment, even though it is, not necessarily his tool. It is a Bible message that we bring, Bible truth that we present, though we shall often find it well to put it into the familiar terms of the everyday life of the one whom we would reach. We must, ourselves, know the Bible through and through. It is the Guide Book to the Way of Life. If, in some exceptional case, one who has not found Christ as Saviour is deeply interested in the Bible, then of course the Scriptures may furnish the very best meeting-ground in the world. But such instances are rare. As a rule, the Bible is to be a goal rather than the beginning of our effort with the unsaved. We must begin with

their present interests; we must not rest until we
ave brought them to such recognition of the Book as
;hall give it unique place in their lives.

The encouragements in the work are greater than Encour-
the difficulties. We have only the Devil working agements
against us; we have God working with us. A fre- ever-
quent surprise is the finding that God has specially present
prepared the way, and that some one whom we approached with reluctance has been longing to be
spoken to. Special difficulties are largely in our own
timorous, Devil-aided imaginations. Rebuffs by those
whom we would win are almost unknown.

The mentally deficient are as much entitled to the The
gospel message as those who have greater temporal mentally
privileges than they, and they are surprisingly ready deficient
and competent to grasp the message and to act upon it.
Surprises are in store for those who, slow to believe
this, will nevertheless put it to the test. Let us never
cheat a childish, helpless soul of the message which
God entrusts to us for that one, and which may bring
into that life the only sunshine it has ever known.

No opportunity is so slight or trifling that it can No op-
safely be passed by. The " trifles " in this work, re- portunity
jected of men, may become cornerstones in life-build- trifling
lngs planned by the Master-Builder. If we admit, of
any opportunity, that it is too trifling to use, we are
sure to lose priceless opportunities. We are especially
in danger of missing the opportunities that are close
at hand,—the commonplace, everyday openings; and
in so doing to overlook the souls nearest to us who
need our help. Opportunity cannot be measured by
man-made rules. " It may be a small matter for you
to speak the one word for Christ that wins a needy

soul—*a small matter to you,* but it is *everything to him.*"

A chief incentive to the persistent doing of this work is the fact that absolutely no other form of effort takes its place. Faithfulness in pulpit or Sunday-school or prayer-meeting is a good accompaniment of it, but never a substitute for it.

Our duty for results

Seeing results in the work may or may not be our privilege. It is our duty to work for results just as long as the result does not appear and the person sought is within our sphere of influence. At times it is an evident duty to urge an immediate decision. Always we ought to make it plain that Jesus Christ accepts at once,—that if there is any delay it is not of his causing. Follow-up work is peculiarly important. It may be supremely important; without it, all our preliminary effort may count for nothing.

Our Lord's nduring purpose

A study of our Lord's ministry on earth shows that the principles here reviewed have the approval of his practise and his teachings. The enduring purpose of Jesus as a man must be our enduring purpose in this work: to get close alongside of men, just as they are, in order to show them that they are dear to us and to our Saviour who would be theirs.

Topics and Questions for Study and Discussion

(To test one's grasp of the contents of the chapter)

1. Mention three distinctive points that characterize individual soul-winning.
2. Briefly summarize the proof of each of those three points.
3. Upon what does efficiency in the work primarily depend?
4. What place should our feelings and our shortcomings have in this work? Why?

5. What do you see in favor of the making of the life-resolve that H. Clay Trumbull made?
6. Upon what should our attention be focused as we prepare to use an opportunity in individual soul-winning?
7. What two effective kinds of bait for taking men alive can you mention?
8. How far may we properly go in identifying ourselves with another's interests for the purpose of winning him to Christ?
9. What is the best way to help a man to settle questions of the details of his personal life and duty?
10. Why are argument and discussion to be barred out of this work?
11. What twofold conviction have we the right to in this work?
12. What place has the Bible in individual soul-winning? Give your reasons fully.
13. Why are the encouragements of the soul-winner greater than his difficulties?
14. How do you account for the fact that the mentally deficient are so ready to grasp the truth of salvation?
15. What is the danger in attempting to discriminate between opportunities in this work?
16. What should be our attitude toward results?
17. What was the enduring purpose of Jesus as a man?

The author will be grateful to readers of this volume who will write him at any time (addressing him at " The Sunday School Times, Philadelphia") concerning their experiences in the field of individual soul-winning, as illustrating any of the principles here presented, or other principles, or in comment upon such questions as the following: page 47, Questions 9, 11, 12; page 61, Question 8; page 88, Questions 6, 8; page 140, Questions 1, 4.

TOPICAL INDEX

194 Topical Index

gar, 178; and blind men, 178; and Canaanitish woman, 178; and centurion of Capernaum, 178; his commendation of the Scribe, 178; and leper of border of Samaria, 178; and sinful woman at house of Simon the Pharisee, 178; and Syrophœnician woman, 178; and the woman in the crowd, 178; emphasizing belief, not doubt, 179; offering proof, 179; seeking points of agreement, 179; his use of Scripture-quoting, 179; withholding proof, 179; his enduring purpose, 180.

Criticism, Christ's use of, 176; has it any place in soul-winning? 83.

"DANGERS of Personal Evangelism;" why not accepted, 55.

Decision? shall we expect immediate, 160 ff.

Defects? what place have our, 57; overlooking others', 176 ff.

Deity of Christ, meeting doubt as to the, 116 ff.

Denouncing others' faults; is it ever justifiable? 83.

Denunciation, Christ's use of, 176.

Difficulty of individual work, 42-46.

Differences of creed, ignoring, 98-101.

Disciples, seven of the twelve individually won, 36, 75 ff., 171; instructed primarily to win, not condemn or denounce, 178, 179.

Discussion, conviction better than, 125 ff.

Dog, apocryphal story of Christ and dead, 177.

Doubts and Doubters," "How to Deal with, 12.

Doubters, Christ and, 175, 176.

Draught of fishes, miraculous, 76-78.

Drinking, settling the question of, 126 ff.

Duty, not a duty to settle others', 125-128.

Drummond's incident of individual work, 165 ff.

Duryea's comment on individual work, 32.

EASY? will individual work grow, 43.

Edinburgh University student, incident of, 165, 166.

Encouragements in the work, 141 ff.

FAITH defined by Bushnell, 94.

Feast of Tabernacles, Christ at the, 174.

Feelings? what place have our, 57.

Finney, evangelistic meetings of, 65.

Fisherman's characteristics in soul-winning, 13.

Fishers of men, disciples made, 76-78.

"Fishin' Jimmy," 12, 13.

Follow-up work, vital importance of, 165; Drummond's incident of, 165, 166; striking incident of, 167.

Freedom to the Jews, Christ offering, 175.

GERMAN rationalist, winning a, 116 ff.

Gough, John B., 153.

Greatest work, individual work the, 31.

Grenfell on reaching souls through bodies, 106, 107.

Guile in individual work, 95.

HACKMAN, Bishop McCabe and the, 153.

Hadley, S. H., "Down in Water Street," 59.

Half-witted, winning the, 145 ff.

Hardest work, individual work the, 42.

Harpoot College, President Browne of, 150.

Horse, story of finding lost, 101.

IMMEDIATE decision? shall we expect, 160 ff.

Imperfections, overlooking others', 176 ff.

Incarnation, meeting doubt as to the, 117 ff.

Incentives to the work, 141 ff.

"Individual Work for Individuals," purpose of the book, 11.

Individual work, Christ's preferred method, 36 ff., 171, 172; what it is, 51; interests as bait, the other man's, 75 ff.; how far afield may we go in, 105, 106; Christ's use of, 173 ff.

"Interruption" in class work, no such thing as, 24.

JABBOK, wrestling match at, 136.

Jacob at Jabbok, 136.

Jacob's well, Christ at, 173, 174.

James won by individual work, 36.

Janitor in theological seminary, winning a, 155.

John won by individual work, 36.

Judas Iscariot, 177.

LAME man, Christ and, 174.

Lazarus' sister, Christ and, 175.

Leper of border of Samaria, Christ and, 178.

Life-resolve in individual work, 69.

Listening important, good, 85.

SCRIPTURE INDEX